NCERT Practice
WORK BOOK

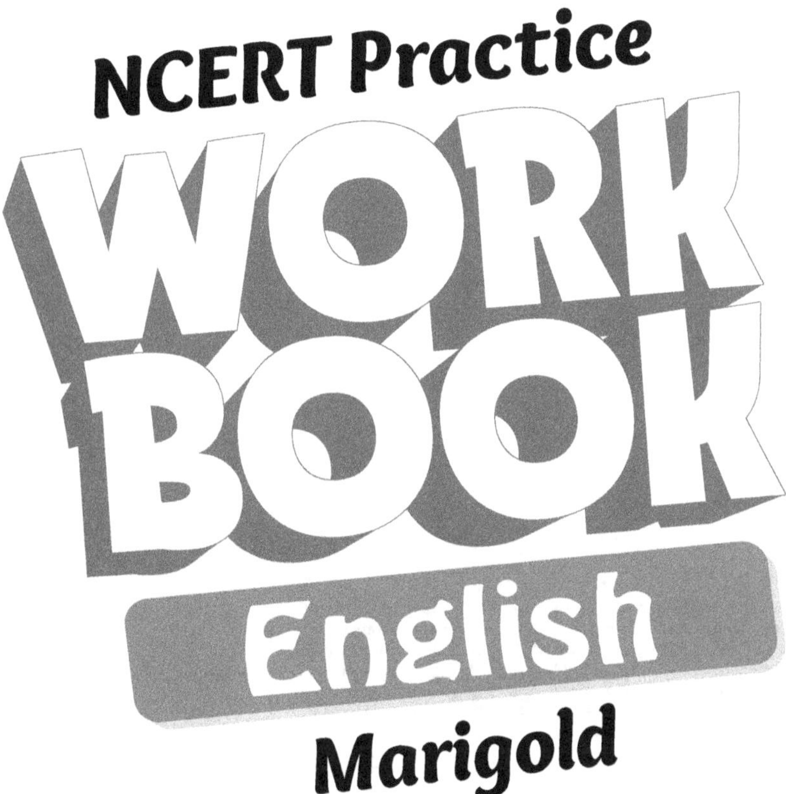

English
Marigold

Emmanuel D'Souza
Gloria D'Souza

arihant
Arihant Prakashan (School Division Series)

✳arihant

Arihant Prakashan (School Division Series)

卐 **Administrative & Production Offices**

Regd. Office
'Ramchhaya' 4577/15, Agarwal Road, Darya Ganj, New Delhi -110002
Tele: 011- 47630600, 43518550

卐 **Head Office**
Kalindi, TP Nagar, Meerut (UP) - 250002
Tel: 0121-7156203, 7156204

卐 **Sales & Support Offices**
Agra, Ahmedabad, Bengaluru, Bareilly, Chennai, Delhi, Guwahati, Hyderabad, Jaipur, Jhansi, Kolkata, Lucknow, Nagpur & Pune.

PO No : TXT-XX-XXXXXXX-X-XX

Published by Arihant Publications (India) Ltd.

For further information about the books published by Arihant, log on to www.arihantbooks.com or e-mail at info@arihantbooks.com

Follow us on    

PRODUCTION TEAM

Publishing Managers
Keshav Mohan, Amit Verma

Project Coordinator
Manju

Project Editor
Sana Fatima

Cover Designer
Bilal Hashmi

Inner Designer
Ankit Saini

Proof Readers
Akash Agarwal

Workbook, Why?

"Knowledge will not be with you for Long Unless You Practice"

This quotation answer the above question 'Workbook, Why ?'
perfectly, i.e Workbooks are made to give the students practice required to achieve
perfection and mastery in the subject. These are the only Workbooks, which are strictly
based on NCERT, the only recommended books by Govt. of India & CBSE (reference
Circular No. Acad-41/2015 dated 20th July 2015).

Given below is the detailed description of Workbook and some of its special features

ONLY COMPLETE WORKBOOK BASED ON NCERT

NCERT textbooks are the only textbooks, which have been prepared according to
National Curriculum Framework, which discourages the idea of rote learning rather
focus on inculcating creativity & initiative in the students to make them participants in
learning not just a receiver of a one-way communication.

Keeping the importance of NCERT textbooks in mind we have prepared this Workbook,
strictly based on NCERT content, this Workbook will complement NCERT by providing
practice on the material given in each chapter of NCERT textbook. This is the only
Workbook, which covers complete Syllabus of English. It has all the four sections;
Literature, Grammar, Writing and Reading.

WORKBOOK- PURPOSE, USE & FEATURES

This Workbook, through its numerous exercises having different variety of questions
covering practical importance of English & Day-to-Day communication, will prove to be
equally useful for both, Classroom and at Home. One more purpose of this Workbook
is to provide the students a systematic practice of the content taught in the class and
what they study in the textbooks.

Some special features of this workbook are

- Complete coverage of all the Sections; Literature, Grammar, Writing and Reading

- Complete coverage of all the Chapters of the NCERT Textbook

- Different variety of questions; Fill in the Blanks, True-False, Matching, Multiple
  Choice Questions, Differentiate between, Define the following, Very Short Answer,
  Short Answer, Long Answer Type etc.

WORKBOOK-DESIGNED TO IMPROVE SUBJECT ABILITIES

All the material given in this workbook is tailored to suit subject content with equal
support on learning, which will surely help students to boost their abilities and
confidence in the subject.

I look forward for the feedback from students, teachers and parents for the further
improvement of the contents of this book. I will try to update the contents according to
your feedback in further editions of this Workbook.

The Publisher

Contents

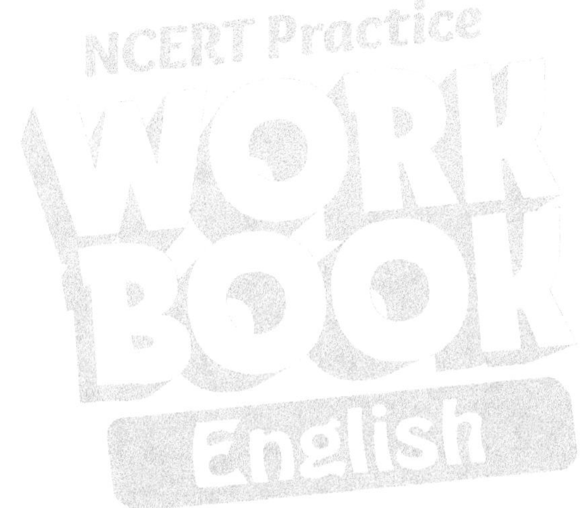

LITERATURE

[Chapter **1**]

Wake up *by C Fletcher*

Text Based Questions

1. Read the extract given below and answer the following questions.

> Wash and dress
> And come on out–
> Everyone is up and about.
> The cow, the horses, the ducks
> And the sheep,
> The tiniest chicken
> Cheep-cheep-cheep
> Wake up!

(i) What is everyone doing?

(ii) What does the poet want us to do?

(iii) Which word in the extract means the same as 'to take bath'?

(a) come on ☐   (b) dress ☐

(c) wash ☐   (d) cheep ☐

(iv) Which of the following is used as an adjective?

(a) dress ☐   (b) up and about ☐

(c) cheep ☐   (d) tiniest ☐

2. State whether the following statements are True (T) or False (F).

(i) It is a sleepy day. ☐

(ii) The birds are chirping. ☐

(iii) The bees are stinging.

(iv) It is too early to get up from bed.

(v) Everyone is awake and out.

Short Answer Type Questions

3. Why does the poet want us to get up?

4. Why does the poet want us to hurry up?

5. Name the animals that the poet has mentioned in the poem.

Language Based Questions

1. Put a (✓) mark on the correct spelling.

(i) Please ☐	Plaese ☐	Pleasae ☐
(ii) Buzing ☐	Buzzing ☐	Buzinng ☐
(iii) Lovely ☐	Lavely ☐	Loevly ☐
(iv) Tinist ☐	Tineist ☐	Tiniest ☐
(v) Chicken ☐	Chiken ☐	Chickeen ☐

2. Match the animals in Column A to the sounds made by them in Column B.

Column A	Column B
(i) Bird	(a) Cheep
(ii) Bee	(b) Sing
(iii) Chicken	(c) Buzz

Neha's Alarm Clock

Adapted from the story by Girija Rani Asthana

Text Based Questions

1. Read the extracts given below and answer the following questions.

I. This alarm clock always rings at six and pulls me out of the bed! It's so unfair .... Oh, how I would love to sleep a little longer in the morning! I wish this clock would forget its job sometimes.

   (i) What happens when the alarm clock rings?

   (ii) What does Neha wish to do?

   (iii) What does Neha wish for the clock?

   (iv) Which word in the extract means the same as 'regularly'?

   (a) alarm ☐   (b) always ☐

   (c) longer ☐   (d) sometimes ☐

II. Even this wish of Neha's comes true. The next morning there is not only no alarm clock, there are no birds either. But there is someone else who does not want her to miss the school bus. Can you guess who it is? The big bright Sun! He fills Neha's room with a warm smile.

   (i) Which wish of Neha comes true?

   (ii) Who doesn't want Neha to miss her school bus?

   (iii) What happens to Neha's room?

(iv) Which word in the extract is the antonym of 'dull'?

(a) true ☐   (b) bright ☐

(c) warm ☐   (d) big ☐

2. State whether the following statements are True (T) or False (F).

(i) The alarm clock rings at six in the morning. ☐

(ii) Neha wants the alarm clock to forget ringing forever. ☐

(iii) Neha is fond of the birds that come to wake her up. ☐

(iv) None of the wishes of Neha comes true. ☐

Short Answer Type Questions

3. How does Neha wake up in the morning?

4. Why is Neha happy?

5. Why does Neha say that she can get up late the next day?

6. What does Neha wish for the Sun? What happens to the Sun on the next day?

7. When does Neha feel that there is no escape?

8. Why does Neha eat her lunch every day at one in the afternoon?

9. Why does Neha sleep at nine every night?

Long Answer Type Question

10. Explain how Neha wakes up on her own.

Language Based Questions

1. Put a (✓) mark on the correct spelling.

(i) Aalarm ☐	Alarm ☐	Alaram ☐
(ii) Unfiar ☐	Unfriar ☐	Unfair ☐
(iii) Smile ☐	Smilie ☐	Simile ☐
(iv) Morining ☐	Morning ☐	Morninng ☐
(v) Escape ☐	Ecsape ☐	Ecscape ☐

2. Match the following words in Column A to their meanings in Column B.

Column A	Column B
(i) Snuggles	(a) get away
(ii) Mutter	(b) ledge
(iii) Escape	(c) ease up
(iv) Window sill	(d) curls up
(v) Relax	(e) mumble

3. In the following sentences, one word has been missed out. Write the missed out word along with the word that comes before it and the word that comes after it.

	Before	Missing Word	After
(i) Oh, how I would love to sleep a longer in the morning!	_______	_______	_______
(ii) So, Neha snores till she hears her voice.	_______	_______	_______
(iii) Ma, who woke me today?	_______	_______	_______
(iv) I want to miss the bus.	_______	_______	_______

4. Write antonyms of the words given below.

(i) Unfair _______________   (ii) Forget _______________

(iii) Fall _______________   (iv) Happy _______________

(v) True _______________

[Chapter 1]

Noses *by Aileen Fisher*

Text Based Questions

1. Read the extracts given below and answer the following questions.

I.
> I looked in the mirror
> and saw in there
> the end of my chin
> and the start of my hair
> and between there
> isn't much space to spare with my nose,
> like a handle, sticking there.

(i) Where did the poet look?

(ii) What did the poet see?

(iii) What is the nose compared to?

(iv) Antonym of 'start' is

(a) go ☐ (b) begin ☐

(c) follow ☐ (d) end ☐

(v) Synonym of 'space' is

(a) outside ☐ (b) volume ☐

(c) room ☐ (d) area ☐

II.
> If ever you want to giggle and shout
> and can't think of what to do it about,
> just look in the mirror and then, no doubt,
> you'll see how funny YOUR nose
> sticks out!

(i) Why should we look in the mirror?

(ii) What is so funny?

(iii) What should one do if there is nothing much to giggle or shout, about?

(iv) Synonym of 'giggle' is

(a) snicker   ☐   (b) chatter   ☐

(c) laugh   ☐   (d) shriek   ☐

2. State whether the following statements are True (T) or False (F).

(i) The poet finds the nose very funny. ☐

(ii) The nose sticks right out where all of it shows. ☐

(iii) The nose is located between the chin and cheeks. ☐

(iv) The nose looks flat in the mirror. ☐

Short Answer Type Questions

3. Why is the nose called funny by the poet?

4. Where is the nose located?

5. What is the purpose of the two little holes?

6. What can we do when we want to have a good laugh?

7. What other suitable title can you suggest for the poem?

Language Based Questions

1. Match the following body parts in Column A to the functions performed by them in Column B.

	Column A		Column B
(i)	Eyes	(a)	Smile
(ii)	Ears	(b)	Eat
(iii)	Nose	(c)	See
(iv)	Lips	(d)	Hear
(v)	Mouth	(e)	Breathe

2. Nose is an important part of the human body. It is used to smell different objects. Identify the smell of the following objects by selecting from the adjectives given in the box.

Sweet, Citrus, Strong, Foul, Chemical, Fragrant

(i) Flowers _______________________

(ii) Garbage _______________________

(iii) Orange _______________________

(iv) Coffee _______________________

(v) Paint _______________________

(vi) Scent _______________________

3. Write the rhyming words for the following.

(i) Nose _______________________

(ii) Shout _______________________

(iii) Hair _______________________

4. Fill in the blanks with correct form of the verb given in brackets.

(i) I ___________ (look/looked) in the mirror at my nose.

(ii) The nose ___________ (is/was) a funny thing according to the poet.

(iii) The nose ___________ (sticks/sticked) like a handle on the face.

(iv) If one ___________ (wanted/wants) to giggle, one can look in the mirror at one's nose.

The Little Fir Tree

Text Based Questions

1. Read the extracts given below and answer the following questions.

I. "Thank you, you have been kind to me. I would like to reward you. Ask for four wishes and I will grant them," said the magician.

   (i) Who is the speaker of these lines?

   (ii) Why did the speaker thank the listener?

   (iii) Who had been kind?

   (iv) Synonym of 'kind' is

      (a) considerate   ☐   (b) ungenerous   ☐

      (c) strong   ☐   (d) soft   ☐

II. "I wish I had glass leaves instead. Men do not steal glass leaves."
The next day its glass leaves shone in the bright sun. "How happy I am!" it said.

   (i) What did the fir tree wish for the third time?

   (ii) What do men not steal?

   (iii) What happened the next day?

   (iv) Simple present tense form of 'shone' is

      (a) shining   ☐   (b) shine   ☐

      (c) shined   ☐   (d) is shining   ☐

2. State whether the following statements are True (T) or False (F).

   (i) Shetty saw an ugly fir tree.

  (ii) Shetty wanted to enjoy the rain.

 (iii) Shetty wanted to reward the tree.

 (iv) The tree was very sad.

  (v) The tree didn't want the birds to make nests on it.

 (vi) A goat ate all the golden leaves.

 (vii) A man stole the glass leaves.

(viii) The golden leaves shone brightly in the Sun.

Short Answer Type Questions

3. What happened suddenly in the beginning of the story?

4. Who looked around for shelter?

5. Who was happy and why?

6. What was the reward?

7. What happened to the green leaves?

8. What did the fir tree wish for the second time?

Long Answer Type Question

9. In the end the tree wishes to have its old needle like leaves back. What lesson do you learn from the story 'The Little Fir Tree'?

Language Based Questions

1. Match the following.

	Column A		Column B
(i)	Shetty	(a)	thief
(ii)	Green leaves	(b)	wind
(iii)	Golden leaves	(c)	needles
(iv)	Glass leaves	(d)	magician
(v)	Fir tree	(e)	goat

2. Correct the spellings of the following words given in the story.

(i) Shletre ___________________   (ii) Rewrad ___________________

(iii) Bidrs ___________________   (iv) Morninng ___________________

(v) Laeves ___________________   (vi) Surpirised ___________________

(vii) Stoel ___________________   (viii) Nedles ___________________

3. Give the antonyms of the following words.

(i) Heavy ___________________   (ii) Fast ___________________

(iii) Happy ___________________   (iv) Wet ___________________

(v) Kind ___________________   (vi) Friend ___________________

(vii) Bright ___________________   (viii) Break ___________________

4. Correct the following sentences.

(i) Shetty were a magician.

____

(ii) It were raining heavily.

____

(iii) The fir tree have leaves like needles.

____

[Chapter 1]

Run! *by Mary Daunt*

Text Based Questions

1. Read the extracts given below and answer the following questions.

I.
> Run in the raindrops!
> Run 'neath the trees!
> Run little races
> With each little breeze!

  (i) What does the poet want the children to run races with?

____

  (ii) The poet wants children to run below ___________________ .

 (iii) The word 'trees' rhymes with the word ___________________ .

II.
> Run down the hillside,
> Run up the lane;
> Run through the meadow,
> Then run back again!

  (i) The poet wants children to run in which three places in this stanza?

____

  (ii) Which will be faster, running down the hillside or running up the lane?

____

 (iii) The word 'meadow' means ___________ .

Short Answer Type Questions

2. Why does the poet ask the children to run back again?

____

3. Suggest another suitable title for the poem.

____

4. Who is the poet of the poem 'Run'?

____

Language Based Questions

1. Put a (✓) mark on the correct spelling.

(i) (a) Raindops	☐	(b) Raindrops	☐
(c) Raindrps	☐	(d) Raiindrop	☐
(ii) (a) Hillside	☐	(b) Hilside	☐
(c) Hillsde	☐	(d) Hllside	☐
(iii) (a) Medow	☐	(b) Meadow	☐
(c) Madow	☐	(d) Meadeow	☐
(iv) (a) Marrey	☐	(b) Mary	☐
(c) Merry	☐	(d) Mery	☐
(v) (a) County	☐	(b) Contry	☐
(c) Country	☐	(d) Contoury	☐

2. Fill in the blanks using the prepositions given in the box.

> *from, to, through, beneath, up, into, in, down, through, to*

(i) The poet asks the children to run away ___________ the city and ___________ the Sun, out ___________ the country.

(ii) The poet says run ___________ the raindrops, ___________ the trees.

(iii) The poet further encourages the children to run ___________ the hillside, ___________ the lane, ___________ the meadow and back again.

(iv) The poet wants the children to be merry all ___________ the day and run ___________ the country.

3. Find word with 'tt', 'ee', 'll' and 'rr' from the poem and write in the given spaces. For example, Tr<u>ee</u>s.

☐	☐
☐	☐

Nasruddin's Aim

Text Based Questions

1. Read the extracts given below and answer the following questions.

I. His friends started laughing. They said, "Hey, Nasruddin! Is this your best aim?"
"Oh, no! Not at all," said Nasruddin, defending himself. "This wasn't my aim. It was Azad's aim."

   (i)   Who started laughing?

   (ii)   Why did Nasruddin defend himself?

   (iii)   Whose aim was it, according to Nasruddin?

   (iv)   Comparative *form* of 'best' is

     (a) good ☐   (b) better ☐

     (c) worse ☐   (d) excellent ☐

II. The arrow hit right on the target!
Everybody stared at Nasruddin, their mouths agape in amazement.
Before anyone could say anything, Nasruddin said triumphantly, "Did you see that? It was my aim!"

   (i)   Why did everyone stare at Nasruddin?

   (ii)   How was Nasruddin feeling?

   (iii)   Whose aim was it?

   (iv)   'Agape' can be replaced with

     (a) wide open ☐   (b) close ☐

     (c) horrible ☐   (d) sad ☐

Short Answer Type Questions

2. What did Nasruddin boast about?

3. What did Nasruddin's friend do when Nasruddin started boasting?

4. What happened when Nasruddin shot the arrow the first time?

5. Why did Nasruddin's friends laugh at him?

6. Did Nasruddin succeed in his second attempt?

7. Whose aim was it the second time around?

8. "Did you see that?" Who said this to whom and why?

Long Answer Type Question

9. Nasruddin missed the target the first time and the second time but the third time, the arrow hit right on the target. Do you think Nasruddin's luck favoured him the third time or was he actually good at archery?

Language Based Questions

1. Match the words in Column A to their meanings in Column B.

Column A	Column B
(i) Chatting	(a) a weapon for shooting
(ii) Boast	(b) object of attack
(iii) Archery	(c) protecting from attack
(iv) Bow	(d) great surprise
(v) Target	(e) happily and proudly
(vi) Defending	(f) talking
(vii) Amazement	(g) shooting with bow and arrow
(viii) Triumphantly	(h) self-praise

2. Change the words using 'LY'.

(i) Triumphant <u>Triumphantly</u> (ii) Skilful ___________

(iii) Immediate ___________ (iv) Pointed ___________

3. Write the noun forms of the following verbs. One has been done for you.

(i) Chatting <u>Chat</u> (ii) Aimed ___________

(iii) Laughing ___________ (iv) Defending ___________

4. Identify the subject and predicate in the following sentences by colouring the subject in green and predicate in orange.

(i) The arrow is sure to hit right on target.

(ii) Nasruddin's friends brought a bow and some arrows.

(iii) Nasruddin took the bow and arrows.

(iv) Nasruddin aimed at the target and shot an arrow.

(v) Nasruddin's friends burst out laughing.

5. Use the words from the box and make your own sentences.

> *Boast, Arrow, Target, Skill, Hit*

(i) ____

(ii) ____

(iii) ____

(iv) ____

(v) ____

[Chapter **1**]

Why?

Text Based Questions

1. Read the extracts given below and answer the following questions.

I.　　　　He wants to know why wood should swim,
　　　　Why lead and marble sink,
　　　　Why sun should shine and wind should blow
　　　　And why we eat and drink.

　(i)　What does the boy want to know about wood?

　(ii)　What does the boy want to know about lead and marble?

　(iii)　The boy wants to know why the __________ shines and why the __________ blows.

　(iv)　Which word in the extract means the same as 'have knowledge'?

　　(a) why ☐　　(b) know ☐

　　(c) eat ☐　　(d) sink ☐

　(v)　Which word in the extract is an antonym of 'float'?

　　(a) wood ☐　　(b) lead ☐

　　(c) sun ☐　　(d) sink ☐

II.　　　　He wants to know what makes the clouds
　　　　And why they cross the sky,
　　　　Why sinks the sun behind the hills
　　　　And why the flowers die.

　(i)　What does the boy want to know about the clouds?

(ii) What does the boy want to know about the sun?

(iii) What happens to the flowers?

(iv) Which word in the extract means the same as 'submerge'?

    (a) make ☐   (b) cross ☐

    (c) sink ☐   (d) die ☐

(v) Antonym of 'die' is

    (a) expire ☐   (b) succumb ☐

    (c) live ☐   (d) perish ☐

2. State whether the following statements are True (T) or False (F).

  (i) The poet knows a curious little boy. ☐

 (ii) The boy wanted to know why we swim. ☐

(iii) The boy wanted to know why we eat and drink. ☐

(iv) The boy wanted to know why the sky hits the clouds. ☐

 (v) The boy wanted to know why the sun sinks behind the hills. ☐

(vi) Some of the boy's questions were not too hard to answer. ☐

Short Answer Type Questions

3. About whom is the poet talking in the poem 'Why'?

4. What does the boy do in the poem 'Why'?

5. What does the boy want to know about the wind?

6. What happens to the sun and the flowers?

7. Were all the questions of the boy answered? Why?

Language Based Questions

1. Put a (✓) mark on the correct spelling.

(i)	Curious	Cureous	Cuerious
(ii)	Mable	Marble	Maarble
(iii)	Cloud	Claud	Clowd
(iv)	Reson	Reaseon	Reason

2. Given below are some words from the poem. Arrange them in dictionary sequence (alphabetical order).

> sink, shine, always, drink, hills, reason, clouds, sun, cross, lead, hard

3. Underline the adjectives in the following phrases.

(i) a curious little boy

(ii) sinking marbles

(iii) shining sun

(iv) blowing wind

(v) dying flowers

4. Write antonyms of the following words.

(i) Little ___________________

(ii) Known ___________________

(iii) Now ___________________

(iv) Behind ___________________

(v) Always ___________________

(vi) Hard ___________________

(vii) Found ___________________

(viii) Answer ___________________

(xi) Why ___________________

5. Give the rhyming words for the following.

(i) Sink ___________________

(ii) Sky ___________________

6. Make your own sentences using each word given in the box.

> Curious, Wood, Swim

(i) ___________________

(ii) ___________________

(iii) ___________________

Alice in Wonderland

Adapted from Alice in Wonderland by Lewis Carroll

Text Based Questions

1. Read the extracts given below and answer the following questions.

I. He had pink eyes and was wearing a blue coat. He took out a big watch from his waistcoat pocket and as he hurried away, he said, "Oh dear, I will be too late!"

She thought there was something very different about this rabbit. It could talk, it wore a red waistcoat and it carried a watch.

(i) Who had pink eyes?

(ii) What did he take out from his pocket?

(iii) What was so different about this rabbit?

(iv) Which word in the extract means the same as 'rushed'?

(a) waistcoat ☐   (b) hurried ☐

(c) late ☐   (d) carried ☐

(v) Antonym of 'different' in the extract is

(a) unique ☐   (b) unlike ☐

(c) similar ☐   (d) distinctive ☐

II. Alice stood up and saw a small door about fifteen inches high. It was too small for her to go through.

She saw a glass table with a golden key on it. She tried the little golden key in the lock and to her delight it fitted! Alice opened the door and looked into the loveliest garden she had ever seen!

(i) What did Alice see?

(ii) Why didn't Alice get through the door?

(iii) What did Alice do with the golden key?

(iv) 'Loveliest' is the superlative form of the adjective

    (a) lovely   ☐   (b) love   ☐

    (c) lover   ☐   (d) lovey   ☐

(v) The word 'pleasure' means the same as the word _________ in the extract.

    (a) stood up   ☐   (b) tried   ☐

    (c) delight   ☐   (d) loveliest   ☐

Short Answer Type Questions

2. Describe the rabbit according to the chapter 'Alice in Wonderland'.

3. What guesses did Alice make about her location?

4. Where did the rabbit disappear? Why couldn't Alice follow him?

5. What did Alice see on standing up from the pile of dry leaves?

6. What did Alice see on the table? What did she do?

Long Answer Type Question

7. What did Alice see when she opened the door? How did she feel?

Language Based Questions

1. Match the words in Column A to their meanings in Column B.

Column A	Column B
(i) Scamper	(a) done more quickly than usual
(ii) Hurried	(b) to become impossible to see any longer
(iii) Popped	(c) to run with quick short steps
(iv) Disappeared	(d) long hairs that grow near the mouth of animals
(v) Whiskers	(e) to go somewhere quickly and unexpectedly

2. Look at the adjectives in the following phrases. Classify them under the headings given below and complete the table.

   (i) A white rabbit

  (ii) Pink eyes

  (iii) A blue coat

  (iv) A big watch

  (v) A red waistcoat

  (vi) A large rabbit hole

  (vii) A pile of dry leaves

  (viii) A small door

  (ix) A glass table

  (x) A little golden key

  (xi) The loveliest garden

  (xii) Beds of bright flowers

  (xiii) Cool fountains

Types of Adjectives

Size	Colour	Quality	Material

3. Read the following and fill in the blanks using suitable prepositions from the box below.

> on, among, by, near, under, through, with, down, into, through, out, from, into

  (i) Alice was lying ____________ a tree.

  (ii) Suddenly, Alice saw a white rabbit scamper ____________ .

  (iii) The rabbit took ____________ a big watch ____________ his waistcoat pocket.

  (iv) The rabbit popped ____________ a large rabbit hole.

  (v) Alice jumped ____________ the rabbit hole too!

4. Rearrange the following words to form meaningful sentences.

  (i) thought/Alice/something/there/was/very/rabbit/different/this/about

  (ii) the/rabbit/Alice/white/followed

  (iii) into/rabbit/Alice/too/the/hole/jumped/!

[Chapter **1**]

Don't be Afraid of the Dark *by Ruskin Bond*

Text Based Questions

1. Read the extracts given below and answer the following questions.

I.
> Don't be afraid of the dark, little one,
> The earth must rest when the day is done.
> The sun must be harsh, but moonlight - never!
> And those stars will be shining forever and ever,

(i)　What does the poet tell us?

____

(ii)　When can the earth rest?

____

(iii)　The moonlight can never be ______________ .

(iv)　The word in the extract which means the same as 'relax' is

(a) little ☐　　　(b) rest ☐　　　(c) harsh ☐　　　(d) earth ☐

(v)　Antonym of 'harsh' in the extract is

(a) sharp ☐　　　(b) gentle ☐　　　(c) rough ☐　　　(d) uneven ☐

II.
> Be friends with the Night, there is nothing to fear,
> Just let your thoughts travel to friends far and near.
> By day, it does seem that our troubles won't cease,
> But at night, late at night, the world is at peace.

(i)　Why should we be friends with the night?

____

(ii)   Where should our thoughts travel?

(iii) What happens in the day?

(iv)   Which word cannot be substituted for 'fear'?
    (a) worry ☐   (b) courage ☐   (c) scare ☐   (d) horror ☐

(v)   Antonym of 'peace' in the extract is _____________ .
    (a) rest ☐   (b) war ☐   (c) happiness ☐   (d) worry ☐

2. State whether the following statements are True (T) or False (F).

  (i)   The poet tells little children not to be afraid of the dark. ☐

 (ii)   The earth requires no rest. ☐

(iii)   The sun is very harsh. ☐

(iv)   The stars shine forever and ever. ☐

 (v)   If we befriend the night, we have nothing to fear. ☐

(vi)   Troubles seem to remain during the day time. ☐

(vii)   The world is never at peace. ☐

Short Answer Type Questions

3. What does the poem 'Don't be Afraid of the Dark' teach us?

4. What happens when the day comes to an end?

5. How can we not fear the night?

6. What happens late at night?

Language Based Questions

1. Match the following words in Column A to their meaning in Column B.

	Column A		Column B
(i)	Afraid	(a)	Take a break
(ii)	Dark	(b)	Unpleasantly rough
(iii)	Rest	(c)	Problems
(iv)	Harsh	(d)	Feeling fear
(v)	Forever	(e)	Come or bring to an end
(vi)	Troubles	(f)	With little or no light
(vii)	Cease	(g)	For always

2. Fill in the blanks with suitable adjectives.

(i) We should not be afraid of the ____________.

(ii) The sun is ____________.

(iii) By the day, everything seems ____________.

(iv) In the night, the world is ____________.

3. Rearrange the letters into meaningful words from the poem.

(i) TAERH ____________ (ii) NSU ____________

(iii) TGOMINOLH ____________ (iv) RTASS ____________

(v) NISRFED ____________ (vi) HIGNT ____________

(vii) VRATEL ____________ (viii) UROLTBES ____________

(ix) ROLWD ____________ (x) AECPE ____________

4. Write the rhyming words of the following words.

(i) One ____________ (ii) Never ____________

(iii) Fear ____________ (iv) Cease ____________

5. Write the antonyms of the following words from the poem.

(i) Afraid ____________ (ii) Dark ____________

(iii) Little ____________ (iv) Rest ____________

(v) Day ____________ (vi) Done ____________

Helen Keller

Text Based Questions

1. Read the extracts given below and answer the following questions.

   I. Helen began to grow wild. She would not let anyone comb her hair. Her clothes were always dirty. She was often angry. Sometimes she even lay on the floor and kicked her feet.

    (i) What changes came in Helen's nature?

    (ii) What did she not allow?

    (iii) How did she express her anger?

    (iv) Antonym of 'wild' is

      (a) tame   ☐   (b) polished   ☐   (c) rude   ☐   (d) serious   ☐

    (v) Find the word in the extract which means the same as 'soiled'.

      (a) comb   ☐   (b) dirty   ☐   (c) angry   ☐   (d) lay   ☐

  II. One day, her teacher made Helen put her hand into running water. Then, she spelt W_A_T_E_R. Suddenly Helen understood that W_A_T_E_R meant something wet, running over her hand. She understood that words were the most important things in the world.

    (i) What did Miss Sullivan do one day?

    (ii) What did Helen understand as the meaning of water?

    (iii) What did Helen understand about words?

(iv) 'Running Water' as used in the extract means

(a) flowing water ☐   (b) stagnant water ☐

(c) fresh water ☐   (d) racing water ☐

(v) Antonym of 'wet' is

(a) soggy ☐   (b) dry ☐

(c) damp ☐   (d) moist ☐

Short Answer Type Questions

2. When and where was Helen born?

3. What happened to the baby one day?

4. What did everyone predict about the baby?

5. Did the baby survive the illness? What happened to her?

6. What was wrong with the baby in the chapter 'Helen Keller'?

7. How did Miss Sullivan spell different words?

8. Who was Miss Sullivan?

Long Answer Type Questions

9. Write a few qualities that Helen possessed.

10. How did Miss Sullivan help Helen in learning?

11. Describe the character of Miss Sullivan.

12. Which incident helped Helen discover the importance of words?

Language Based Questions

1. Unscramble the letters to make words with the help of the clues given in brackets.

   (i) UMESMR (A season)

  (ii) LEAHTYH (Physically fit)

 (iii) SNLILES (Synonym of sickness)

  (iv) ROYSR (To apologise)

   (v) ACTEREH (A guide or mentor)

2. Match the two parts of sentences given in Column A and B. Combine each pair of sentence using the conjunction 'and,' 'but,' 'or' to form a single sentence and write in the space below.

Column A	Column B
(i) Helen's parents loved her dearly	(a) she was not the same after illness.
(ii) Helen survived the illness	(b) she was kind.
(iii) Helen could not see	(c) she did not understand what she was doing.
(iv) Helen copied her teacher and spelt DOLL	(d) they named her Helen Keller.
(v) Miss Sullivan was strict	(e) she could not hear.

3. Match the words in Column A with their meanings in Column B.

Column A		Column B	
(i)	Dearly	(a)	a disease of the body
(ii)	Healthy	(b)	very much
(iii)	Illness	(c)	expecting people to obey rules or to do what you say
(iv)	Smart	(d)	of great significance or value
(v)	Problem	(e)	having good health
(vi)	Wild	(f)	behaving in an uncontrolled or violent way
(vii)	Strict	(g)	intelligent
(viii)	Important	(h)	a situation that causes difficulties

4. Write the comparative and superlative form of the adjectives given below.

	Adjective	Comparative	Superlative
(i)	Healthy	_____________	_____________
(ii)	Small	_____________	_____________
(iii)	High	_____________	_____________
(iv)	Good	_____________	_____________
(v)	Little	_____________	_____________
(vi)	Poor	_____________	_____________
(vii)	Thick	_____________	_____________
(viii)	Smart	_____________	_____________
(ix)	Wild	_____________	_____________
(x)	Dirty	_____________	_____________

5. Write the antonyms of the following words.

(i) Healthy _____________   (ii) Small _____________

(iii) Love _____________   (iv) High _____________

[Chapter **1**]

Hiawatha   *by HW Longfellow*

Text Based Questions

1. Read the extract given below and answer the questions that follow.

> Learned their names and all their secrets,
> How the beavers built their lodges,
> Where the squirrels hid their acorns,
> How the reindeer ran so swiftly,
> Why the rabbit was so timid,

(i) What did Hiawatha learn?

____

(ii) Where did the beavers live?

____

(iii) What did the squirrels hide?

____

(iv) Synonym of 'swiftly' is

(a) sluggishly ☐　　(b) quickly ☐　　(c) racingly ☐　　(d) slowly ☐

(v) Antonym of 'timid' is

(a) fearless ☐　　(b) humble ☐　　(c) weak ☐　　(d) coward ☐

Short Answer Type Questions

2. Answer the following questions briefly after reading the poem.

(i) What was the name of the young boy?

____

(ii) What did Nokomis teach him?

(iii) What could the young boy do when he grew up?

(iv) What did the young boy learn about animals?

(v) What qualities did the reindeer and the rabbit possess?

(vi) Suggest another title for the poem 'Hiawatha'.

(vii) Who are Hiawatha's chickens and his brothers?

3. Complete the following table about what the following animals did in the poem.

Name of the Animal	What the animal did
(i) Beaver	_______________
(ii) Squirrel	_______________
(iii) Reindeer	_______________
(iv) Rabbit	_______________

4. Write one sentence about each of the following with reference to the poem.

(i) Little Hiawatha

(ii) Birds

(iii) Beavers

(iv) Summer

(v) Winter

(vi) Rabbit

Language Based Questions

1. Match the following words in Column A to their meanings in Column B.

Column A		Column B	
(i)	Secret	(a)	not having courage or confidence
(ii)	Wigwam	(b)	known about by only a few people and kept hidden from others
(iii)	Beast	(c)	home
(iv)	Beaver	(d)	a dwelling with a round or pointed roof
(v)	Lodge	(e)	animal
(vi)	Acorn	(f)	a North-American animal with thick fur and a wide flat tail
(vii)	Timid	(g)	the nut of the oak tree

2. Write antonyms of the following.

(i) Top ____________   (ii) Hide ____________

(iii) Build ____________   (iv) Swift ____________

3. You have read about a few animals in the poem. Now write where they live.

(i) Birds live in ____________ .   (ii) Beavers live in ____________ .

(iii) Rabbits live in ____________ .

4. Homophones are words with similar sounds but different meanings or spellings. Read the following words given below and write at least one homophone for each of the following.

(i) All ____________   (ii) Deer ____________

(iii) Meet ____________   (iv) Their ____________

(v) Build ____________

5. Using the words given in the box, make your own sentences.

> Bird, Beast, Built, Learn, Timid

(i) ____

(ii) ____

(iii) ____

(iv) ____

(v) ____

The Scholar's Mother Tongue

Adapted from Akbar and Birbal stories

Text Based Questions

1. Read the extracts given below and answer the following questions.

I. The Pundit could speak many languages fluently. He was so fluent that no one could find out what his mother tongue was. He challenged everybody at the court to name his mother tongue. When everyone failed, the challenge was taken up by Birbal.

(i) What were the courtiers unable to guess?

(ii) What did the Pundit challenge the courtiers with?

(iii) Antonym of 'failed' is

(a) demoted ☐ (b) wrong ☐ (c) reached ☐ (d) succeeded ☐

(iv) Find the word in the passage which means the same as 'smooth'.

(a) challenged ☐ (b) taken up ☐ (c) fluent ☐ (d) court ☐

II. That night, Birbal went quietly to the Pundit's room when he was asleep. He whispered into the Pundit's ear and tickled it with a feather. The Pundit, half awake, cried out suddenly and shouted out words in his mother tongue.

(i) What did Birbal do at night?

(ii) How did Birbal disturb the Pundit?

(iii) How did the Pundit react?

(iv) Find the word in the passage which means the same as 'murmured'.

(a) whispered ☐ (b) quietly ☐ (c) asleep ☐ (d) tickled ☐

(v) Find the synonym of 'screamed' in the passage.

(a) whispered ☐ (b) tickled ☐ (c) cried ☐ (d) awake ☐

2. Read the following sentences carefully. Some of the sentences are incorrect. Put a ☒ and correct them and rewrite them in the space provided. Put a ☑ in front of the correct sentences.

(i) The learned Pundit told the king and his courtiers that he had mastery over many different languages. ☐

(ii) The Pundit was so fluently that no one could find out what his mother tongue is. ☐

(iii) Birbal whisked into the Pundit's nose and tickled it with a leaf. ☐

(iv) Birbal informed the king how he had gone to the Pundit's room to find the truth. ☐

Short Answer Type Questions

3. Who took up the challenge and why?

4. In whose court was Birbal a courtier?

5. How did the Pundit react when the truth was out?

6. How do people react in times of difficulty?

Long Answer Type Questions

7. Do you think Birbal was a clever man? If yes, why?

8. Who visited the court of Akbar? What was his special ability and what did he challenge the courtiers to?

Language Based Questions

1. Circle the subject and underline the predicate in the following sentences.
   (i) A learned Pundit once visited the court of Akbar.
   (ii) The Pundit could speak many laguages fluently.
   (iii) Birbal went quietly to the Pundit's room when he was asleep.

2. Read the following sentences and fill in the blanks with the correct preposition.
   (i) The Pundit had mastery _____________ many different languages.

   (ii) He challenged everybody _____________ the court to name his mother tongue.

   (iii) When everyone failed, Birbal took _____________ the challenge.

   (iv) Birbal quietly went _____________ the Pundit's room _____________ night.

   (v) He whispered _____________ the Pundit's ear and tickled it _____________ a feather.

3. Read the following extract taken from the chapter carefully. There are many mistakes in punctuation. Correct the mistakes and rewrite the paragraph.

king akbar then asked birbal, how did you find the truth.

birbal answered in times of difficulty a person speaks only in his mother tongue. he also told the king how he had gone to the Pundits room at night to find out the truth.

[Chapter 1]

A Watering Rhyme *by PA Ropes*

Text Based Questions

1. Read the extract given below and answer the following questions.

> Water at the roots;
> Flowers keep their mouths where
> We should wear our boots.
> Soak the earth around them,
> Then through all the heat
> The flowers will have water
> For their thirsty 'feet'!

(i) Where should we water the flowers?

____

(ii) In the stanza, what does 'feet' refer to?

____

(iii) Find the word in the extract which means the same as 'drench'.

(a) water ☐　　(b) soak ☐　　(c) thirsty ☐　　(d) roots ☐

(iv) Antonym of 'heat' is

(a) cold ☐　　(b) warm ☐　　(c) torrid ☐　　(d) sultry ☐

Short Answer Type Questions

2. When should we water the flowers?

____

3. What makes the flower die?

____

4. What is the position of the sun at noon?

5. Why do flowers need water?

Language Based Questions

1. Match the words in Column A with their meanings in Column B.

	Column A		**Column B**
(i)	Watering	(a)	the part of a plant that grows under the ground
(ii)	Noonday	(b)	to make something completely wet
(iii)	Roots	(c)	pouring water
(iv)	Boots	(d)	at noon
(v)	Soak	(e)	a type of shoe

2. Rearrange the following letters to make meaningful words.

(i) NNIMROG __________   (ii) EOWFRL __________

(iii) OYNDAON __________   (iv) SUOTMH __________

(v) OTBSO __________   (vi) TAREH __________

3. Write the antonyms of the following words.

(i) Early __________   (ii) High __________

(iii) Morning __________   (iv) Die __________

4. Write the rhyming words for the following.

(i) Hour __________   (ii) High __________

(iii) Roots __________   (iv) Heat __________

5. Unjumble the names of the flowers.

(i) EORS _ _ _ E   (ii) SOTUL L _ _ _ _

(iii) YILL L _ _ _   (iv) SAMNIEJ J _ _ _ _ _ E

The Giving Tree

Adapted from 'The Giving Tree' by Shel Silverstein

Text Based Questions

1. Read the extracts given below and answer the following questions.

I. The boy happily plucked the apples and carried them away. The tree was also happy. But the boy stayed away for a long time and the tree was sad. One day, the boy came back and the tree shook with joy.

(i) What did the boy do?

____

(ii) What happened when the boy came back?

____

(iii) Find the word in the extract which means the opposite of 'sorrow'.

(a) happy ☐   (b) stayed ☐

(c) joy ☐   (d) sad ☐

(iv) The meaning of 'plucked' in the extract is

(a) pull ☐   (b) take out ☐

(c) remove ☐   (d) take hold and remove ☐

II. The young man cut the trunk of the tree and sailed away in a boat. The tree was left only with a stump.

And after a long time the young man came back again. Now he was an old man but the tree recognised him.

(i) What did the young man do?

____

(ii) What happened to the tree?

____

(iii) What happened to the young man?

____

(iv) Find out the word from the extract which is a synonym of 'stem'.

(a) tree ☐　　(b) trunk ☐　　(c) stump ☐　　(d) boat ☐

(v) Antonym of 'recognised' is

(a) recalled ☐　　(b) remembered ☐　　(c) forgot ☐　　(d) missed ☐

Short Answer Type Questions

2. How did the boy have fun in the play 'The Giving Tree' ?

3. How did the tree help the boy to earn money ?

4. What three things did the tree give to the little boy?

5. How and why did the boy build his house ?

6. Where was the boy going ? How did the tree help him ?

Long Answer Type Question

7. It can be said that the author rightly named the tree as 'The Giving Tree' which gave away everything it had? How did the tree change by the end of the story?

Language Based Questions

1. Match the subjects in Column A to the predicates in Column B to make meaningful sentences.

Column A	Column B
(i) The boy	(a) was happy to give its shade.
(ii) The tree	(b) cut the trunk of the tree and sailed away in a boat.

	Column A		Column B
(iii)	The young man	(c)	wanted a quiet place to sit and rest.
(iv)	The old man	(d)	climbed the trunk and swung from the branches of the tree.
(v)	The old stump	(e)	had lost its apples, branches and trunk.

2. Choose the correct conjunction from the options given and fill in the blanks.

(i) Once there was a tree ______________ and/but/or it loved a little boy.

(ii) The boy grew older ______________ but/ or /and went away.

(iii) The boy happily plucked the apples ______________ but/and/or carried them away.

(iv) The tree was very happy ______________ but/or/and the boy stayed away for a long time.

(v) The young man was an old man now ______________ and/or/but the tree recognised him.

3. Fill in the blanks with the correct prepositions.

to   in   by   to   with   up   on   from

(i) But time went ______________ and the boy grew older and went away.

(ii) One day the boy came ______________ the tree.

(iii) The tree asked him to climb ______________ its trunk and swing ______________ its branches.

(iv) The boy was too big ______________ climb and play.

(v) The tree asked him to pluck its apples and sell them ______________ the market.

(vi) The boy was going ______________ a business trip.

(vii) He cut off the trunk of the tree and the tree was left only ______________ a stump.

4. Look at the table given below and write the comparative and superlative degree of the adjectives given below.

S No	Positive Degree	Comparative Degree	Superlative Degree
(i)	Small	________________	________________
(ii)	Funny	________________	________________
(iii)	Delicious	________________	________________
(iv)	Tired	________________	________________
(v)	Happy	________________	________________

The Donkey *by Margaret S Russell*

Text Based Questions

1. Read the extract given below and answer the following questions.

> I'd find a little hay
> And give him some corn,
> Then he'd be the best donkey
> That ever was born.

(i) Name the two things that the poet wants to feed the donkey.

(ii) What will happen when the donkey is fed?

(iii) Antonym of 'best' is

(a) bad ☐ (b) not good ☐

(c) better ☐ (d) worst ☐

Short Answer Type Questions

2. What would the poet do if the donkey wouldn't go?

3. How would the donkey become the best donkey?

Language Based Questions

1. Put a (✓) mark on the correct spelling

(i)	donkiy ☐	donkey ☐	dankey ☐
(ii)	wollop ☐	wallap ☐	wallop ☐
(iii)	hey ☐	hay ☐	heya ☐
(iv)	little ☐	liittlle ☐	litle ☐
(v)	carn ☐	corn ☐	con ☐

2. Fill in the blanks with correct form of the verb.

If I (i) _____________ (have/had) a donkey, I (ii) _____________ (will/would) never wallop him. I (iii) _____________ (will find/would find) a little hay to feed him. I (iv) _____________ (will give/would give) him some corn to eat. He (v) _____________ (will/would) be the best donkey ever.

3. Give the rhyming words of the following.

(i) Go _____________   (ii) Corn _____________

4. Using the words given in the box, make your own sentences.

> *Wallop, Little, Hay, Corn, Donkey*

(i) ____

(ii) ____

(iii) ____

(iv) ____

(v) ____

5. Write five lines on the topic 'My Pet'.

(i) ____

(ii) ____

(iii) ____

(iv) ____

(v) ____

[Chapter **1**]

Books

Text Based Questions

1. Read the extract given below and answer the following questions.

> I opened one up
> And sat down to look;
> The pictures told stories!
> What a wonderful book!

(i) What did the poet do?

(ii) How did the poet understand the stories in the book?

(iii) What kind of a book was it?

(iv) Antonym of 'wonderful' is

   (a) awful   (b) pleasant

   (c) terrific   (d) cool

(v) 'The pictures told stories!' In this sentence, 'pictures' is which part of speech?

   (a) Adjective   (b) Noun

   (c) Verb   (d) None of these

Short Answer Type Questions

2. What did the library door say?

3. What did the poet in the poem 'Books' see on opening the library door?

4. What kinds of books were there?

Language Based Questions

1. Match the things mentioned in Column A to the place they belong in Column B.

Column A		Column B	
(i)	Books	(a)	Toy shop
(ii)	Students	(b)	Library
(iii)	Toys	(c)	Zoo
(iv)	Animals	(d)	Garden
(v)	Flowers	(e)	School

2. Circle the subject and underline the predicate in the following sentences.
  (i) The poet saw a lot of books in the library.
  (ii) The books were kept on the shelves.
  (iii) Some books were kept in a standing position.
  (iv) The poet opened one of the books.
  (v) The pictures in the book were very interesting.

3. Complete the following sentences using your own imagination.
  (i) Books are_________________________________.
  (ii) In a library_________________________________.
  (iii) We find books_________________________________.
  (iv) There are_________________________________.
  (v) I like_________________________________.

4. Write antonyms of the following words.
  (i) Come _______________   (ii) Open _______________
  (iii) Wide _______________   (iv) Tall _______________

Going to Buy a Book

by Rukmini Banerji

Text Based Questions

1. Read the extract given below and answer the following questions.

> We ran home to our grandfather.
> We climbed on his bed.
> He put his arms around us and then
> We read, and read, and read.

  (i) Where did the children go?

  (ii) What did they do?

  (iii) What did grandfather do?

  (iv) Find the word in the extract which means the same as 'moved up'.

      (a) ran ☐   (b) climbed ☐   (c) put ☐   (d) bed ☐

  (v) Simple present form of 'ran' is ___________.

Short Answer Type Questions

2. What did grandfather give and to whom?

3. What did grandfather want the children to do?

4. Who were happy and why in the story 'Going to Buy a Book'?

5. With whom did the children go in the story 'Going to Buy a Book'?

6. Why did the children go there?

7. Why did the children decide to go to the small shop?

8. How did the man in the small bookshop help the children?

Long Answer Type Questions

9. Which book did the girl buy and why?

10. Which book did the boy decide to buy and why?

11. How did the grandfather treat the children?

12. How did the children choose the books they wanted to buy?

Language Based Questions

1. Choose the appropriate adjective from the box below and fill in the blanks.

> *quiet, fat, happy, big, small*

   (i) The children were very ___________.

  (ii) They decided to go to a ___________ shop.

 (iii) The bookshop was very ___________ as there was no sound.

 (iv) The girl bought a ___________ book with many stories.

  (v) The boy bought a ___________ book with many pictures.

2. Complete the sentences by using the determiners given in the box.

> *these, many, some, those, both, two, one*

   (i) ___________ day, grandfather gave the children ___________ money.

  (ii) ___________ the children were very happy.

 (iii) ___________ of them loved to read.

 (iv) Just the ___________ of them went to the bookshop.

  (v) The bookshop had ___________ books.

 (vi) "___________ books are about animals", said the man in the shop.

3. Fill in the blanks with correct prepositions.

   (i) The children loved ___________ read.

  (ii) The man ___________ the shop helped the children.

 (iii) The man smiled ___________ them.

 (iv) The children picked some books and sat ___________ the floor.

  (v) They came home and climbed ___________ their grandfather's bed.

[Chapter **1**]

The Naughty Boy   *by John Keats*

Text Based Questions

1. Read the extract given below and answer the following questions.

> There was a naughty boy,
> And a naughty boy was he.
> He ran away to Scotland,
> The people there to see -
> Then he found
> That the ground
> Was as hard,
> That a yard
> Was as long,

(i) What kind of a boy was he?

____

(ii) Where did he run away to?

____

(iii) How was the ground?

____

(iv) Which word from the extract means the same as 'rocky'?

   (a) naughty ☐   (b) ground ☐   (c) hard ☐   (d) yard ☐

(v) Antonym of 'long' is

   (a) tall ☐   (b) short ☐   (c) remote ☐   (d) towering ☐

2. State whether the following statements are True (T) or False (F).

(i) There wasn't a naughty boy. ☐

(ii) He ran away to Scotland. ☐

(iii) He found the ground was hard there. ☐

(iv) He found merry songs there. ☐

(v) He found wooden doors in England. ☐

(vi) He kept wondering about his shoes. ☐

Short Answer Type Questions

3. Why did the naughty boy run away?

4. Was the quality of lead different in the new country?

5. What did the naughty boy find in the new country?

Language Based Questions

1. Put a (✓) mark on the correct spelling.

(i) Scotland ☐	Sotland ☐	Scotand ☐
(ii) Noughty ☐	Nauhty ☐	Naughty ☐
(iii) Mery ☐	Merry ☐	Marry ☐
(iv) Forscore ☐	Furscore ☐	Fourscore ☐
(v) Wondered ☐	Wondred ☐	Wandered ☐

2. The poet has made use of a lot of adjectives to describe the following words. Find those adjectives from the poem and write in the space provided.

(i) Boy _______________ (ii) Ground _______________

(iii) Yard _______________ (iv) Song _______________

(v) Cherry _______________ (vi) Lead _______________

Pinocchio
Adapted from the story of Pinocchio

Text Based Questions

1. Read the extracts given below and answer the questions that follow.

I. He set to work, and as the puppet boy took shape, the old man said, "He must have a name. I will call him Pinocchio."

As soon as he finished making the eyes, the carpenter was amazed to see them move. Before the mouth was made, it began to laugh.

(i) What did the carpenter do with the piece of wood?

(ii) What did he call him?

(iii) What happened as soon as the eyes were made?

(iv) Synonym of 'amazed' is

(a) impressed ☐ (b) surprised ☐ (c) touched ☐ (d) thrilled ☐

(v) Antonym of 'laugh' is

(a) cry ☐ (b) giggle ☐ (c) glad ☐ (d) happy ☐

II. Pinocchio told him a lie … and his nose started growing longer and longer.
Each time he was rude to someone or told a lie, his nose grew longer. Finally Pinocchio said, "I'm glad to be a real boy. I'll never lie again."

(i) Who told a lie and to whom?

(ii) Why did his nose grow longer?

(iii) Who was happy and why?

(iv) Find the word in the extract which means the same as 'impolite'.

  (a) long ☐   (b) grew ☐   (c) lie ☐   (d) rude ☐

(v) Antonym of 'glad' is

  (a) smile ☐   (b) unhappy ☐   (c) depression ☐   (d) dejection ☐

Short Answer Type Questions

2. What did the old carpenter buy?

3. What was so astonishing about his puppet?

4. How did Pinocchio play a trick on the carpenter?

5. What did Pinocchio do in the school?

6. What did the carpenter do when he saw that Pinocchio's legs were stiff?

7. What promise did Pinocchio make in the end?

Long Answer Type Question

8. Describe how the carpenter made Pinocchio's body parts one after the other.

Language Based Questions

1. Fill in the blanks using the prepositions given in the box.

   (i) It was a strange piece __________ wood.

  (ii) As soon as the carpenter's back was turned, the puppet put __________ its tongue.

 (iii) Pinocchio did nothing __________ the school.

 (iv) He often ran away __________ school.

2. Fill in the blanks with the correct form of the verb by selecting from those given in brackets.

   (i) The old carpenter __________ (hear/heard) a little laughing voice.

  (ii) The old man __________ (set/sets) to work.

 (iii) The old man __________ (name/named) the puppet Pinocchio.

 (iv) The carpenter __________ (decide/decided) to __________ (sent/send) Pinocchio to school.

  (v) Whenever Pinocchio __________ (tell/told) a lie, his nose grew longer.

3. Write the noun forms of the following verbs. One has been done for you.

   (i) Laughing - Laughter   (ii) Puzzled __________

 (iii) Began __________   (iv) Grew __________

  (v) Decided __________

4. Write antonyms of the following words.

   (i) Rude __________   (ii) Strange __________

 (iii) Amazed __________   (iv) Long __________

  (v) Stop __________   (vi) Stiff __________

 (vii) Lie __________

5. Add subjects to these predicates to make meaningful sentences.

   (i) __________ used his plane on the queer piece of wood.

  (ii) __________ began to laugh.

 (iii) __________ did nothing but look for fun.

 (iv) __________ was glad to be a real boy.

GRAMMAR

[Chapter **1**]

Adjectives

1. Look at the following sets of adjectives. In every set only one of them is correct. Put (✓) in the box if the word is correct and (✗) if the word is wrong.

(i) unactive ☐	inactive ☐	imactive ☐
(ii) immodest ☐	unmodest ☐	inmodest ☐
(iii) untidy ☐	imtidy ☐	intidy ☐
(iv) inmovable ☐	immovable ☐	unmovable ☐
(v) invalid ☐	imvalid ☐	unvaliid ☐

2. Fill in the blanks with appropriate adjectives based on the sentences given.

(i) Her face is aglow with joy.

She has a ___________ face.

(ii) The baby is asleep.

Don't disturb the ___________ baby.

(iii) The boy set the haystack ablaze.

Did you see the ___________ haystack?

(iv) Geeta was ashamed of her brother's behaviour in class.

What ___________ behaviour!

(v) Something seems amiss! I can't find my spectacles.

Has anyone seen my ___________ spectacles?

3. Use the correct adjectives from the box given below to fill in the blanks.

> *awful, beautiful, unfortunate, ashamed, proud*

A stag, drinking water by the side of a pool, saw his own reflection in it. He thought to himself,

"My horns are so (i) ___________ but my long, thin legs are so (ii) ___________ that I am quite

(iii) ___________ of anyone seeing them". Just then came some hunters. The stag tried to run away but his horns got stuck in the branches of a tree. The hunters killed him. As he was dying, he said, "Oh, I am so (iv) ______________ . I was (v) ____________ of my horns but they are the cause of my death. I didn't like my legs but my legs could have saved me."

4. Fill in the blanks using the superlative form of the adjectives given in brackets.

   (i) The bear lived in the ____________ (*far*) corner of the jungle.

  (ii) She sat in the ____________ (*comfortable*) seat near the window.

 (iii) She is my ____________ (*good*) friend.

 (iv) I want the ____________ (*beautiful*) rose in the world.

  (v) This is my ____________ (*old*) brother.

5. Complete the blanks with the correct positive, comparative or superlative forms.

   (i) Sahiba is the ____________ athlete in our town. (*good, better, best*)

  (ii) But she is the ____________ dancer I have ever known. (*bad, worse, worst*)

 (iii) Mahima has an ____________ brother called Arun. (*old, elder, eldest*)

 (iv) Garima studies in a private school which has a building even ____________ than the Science Museum. (*modern, more modern, most modern*)

  (v) She thinks rugby is the ____________ sport in the world. (*exciting, more exciting, most exciting*)

6. Use the suffixes in the box to change the following nouns into adjectives.

-ish	-ous	-ing	-y	-able
-ive	-ic	-ly	-ed	-en

How many different adjectives can you make with each noun ?

   (i) expense ____

  (ii) scene ____

 (iii) comfort ____

 (iv) friend ____

  (v) wood ____

Articles

1. Fill in the blanks with 'a', 'an' or 'the'. If no article is required, mark 'X'.

   (i)   This is _____________ picture of _____________ elephant.

   (ii) Are you doing _____________ project on _____________ deserts of India?

   (iii) Have you ever seen _____________ penguin run?

   (iv) _____________ policeman caught _____________ robber on the road. But when he searched

         _____________ robber, he found nothing.

   (v)   _____________ boy, who won the first prize is my neighbour.

2. Correct the following sentences by adding, removing or changing articles where required.

   (i)   Which is a largest city in Canada?

   (ii) We live in a old house near station.

   (iii) India is the very big country.

   (iv) What is a name of this village?

   (v)   Don't forget to turn off an light when you go out.

3. Read the following passage on the sports legend Sachin Tendulkar and fill in the correct articles.

   Sachin Tendulkar is one of (i) _____________ best batsmen the world has ever seen. Sachin

   made his debut in (ii) _____________ year 1989 against Pakistan. He was only (iii) _____________

   teenager then. Sachin was up against one of the strongest teams in (iv) _____________ world.

   But (v) _____________ young Sachin played with a lot of determination. In 1990, he became

   (vi) _____________ second youngest player to have scored (vii) _____________ test century at

   Old Trafford.

4. Read the following conversation about a famous tourist place and fill in the blanks with 'a', 'an' or 'the'.

Alok   : Last winter we went to (i) ____________ Ajanta caves in Maharashtra.

Aaditya : That must have been fun!

Alok   : Oh yes, it was! (ii) ____________ caves have many Buddhist paintings and sculptures.

Aaditya : Do you know (iii) ____________ place which is (iv) ____________ World Heritage site?

Alok   : Yes, I do. Our guide told us that many of (v) ____________ sculptures were on

Gautama Buddha's life and (vi) ____________ Jataka tales.

5. Read the passage given below and add appropriate articles where needed.

Once upon a time, there lived in Japan old couple who had tamed sparrow. Everyday he came to be fed, and sat on their shoulder as though he was sitting on forest tree.

One day, old couple was in kitchen garden when their bad-tempered neighbour called out, 'You won't see your precious sparrow again. He ate my rice, and I've cut his tongue out.' cruel woman laughed. poor couple was filled with sorrow. They wandered into woods calling bird. By and by, they came to clearing. There stood most beautiful little house, only few feet high. sparrow came out of house! couple was overjoyed.

6. In the following passage one word has been omitted from each line. Write the omitted word along with the word that comes before and after it.

	Before	Missing	After
(i) Krishna was born in small village called	__________	__________	__________
(ii) Raghurajpur near temple town of Puri in Odisha.	__________	__________	__________
(iii) He had happy childhood, growing up	__________	__________	__________
(iv) among trees and green fields of his village. His	__________	__________	__________
(v) mother was simple and pious woman who loved him dearly.	__________	__________	__________

Verbs and Tenses

1. Select the verb that best suits the sentence.

    (i) Sugandha is ___________ at the annual day celebrations of the school.

       (a) studying   ☐   (b) mocking   ☐

       (c) dancing   ☐   (d) laughing   ☐

    (ii) Shushant is ___________ his friend climb the pole.

       (a) dancing   ☐   (b) ignoring   ☐

       (c) watching   ☐   (d) gazing   ☐

    (iii) The juggler is ___________ the balls in the air and catching them.

       (a) moving   ☐   (b) throwing   ☐

       (c) playing   ☐   (d) picking   ☐

    (iv) Ravya is ___________ the suitcase for her holiday.

       (a) packing   ☐   (b) closing   ☐

       (c) opening   ☐   (d) stuffing   ☐

    (v) Vasu is ___________ a lovely story written by Khushwant Singh.

       (a) listening   ☐   (b) reading   ☐

       (c) finding   ☐   (d) writing   ☐

2. Fill in the blanks with the appropriate verbs from the box given below.

> burnt, stolen, read, filled, bitten, took, washed, answered

    (i) One day a summer flood ___________ the hare out of the burrow.

    (ii) The policeman thought that some men had ___________ his bicycle.

    (iii) The child may be ___________ by the mongoose.

    (iv) They ___________ him to the nearest village.

    (v) Have you ___________ all the questions?

    (vi) A fire ___________ the house down.

3. Fill in the blanks using simple past tense of the verbs given in brackets.

A father one day (i) ___________ (*ask*) his two daughters:

'What is the sweetest thing in the world?'

'Sugar' (ii) ___________ (*answer*) the elder daughter.

'Salt', (iii) ___________ (*reply*) his younger daughter.

The father (iv) ___________ (*think*) that his younger daughter was joking. He (v) ___________ (*get*) angry and (vi) ___________ (*throw*) her out of the house.

The younger daughter later (vii) ___________ (*marry*) a prince. She (viii) ___________ (*invite*) her father for the wedding feast. There (ix) ___________ (*be*) no salt in any of the dishes.

Her father could not eat anything. He then (x) ___________ (*realise*) how important salt was.

4. Choose the most appropriate form of the verb from the options given below.

(i) The policeman ___________ the thief red-handed.

    (a) catch   (b) caught

    (c) is caught   (d) catching

(ii) The whole day yesterday the boys ___________ to the cricket commentary.

    (a) listen   (b) will listen

    (c) has listened   (d) listened

(iii) I ___________ Spanish from my friend who ___________ in Spain.

    (a) learnt, lives   (b) learnt, living

    (c) learn, live   (d) had learnt, live

(iv) I ___________ a number of detective novels when I was a child.

    (a) reading   (b) was read

    (c) had read   (d) have reading

(v) I ___________ the assignment before the bell ___________ .

    (a) had finished, rang   (b) had finished, had rung

    (c) finished, had rung   (d) finish, will ring

Chapter 4

Nouns and Pronouns

A. Nouns

1. Read the following sentences and underline the proper nouns.

   (i) Ravi is going to watch the movie Spiderman Returns tomorrow.

  (ii) The movie is running at the new theatre, Cinemax.

 (iii) Cinemax is one of the best theatres in Delhi.

 (iv) This week, Ravi's school is closed for Diwali.

  (v) The movie will be on till next Friday.

 (vi) Ravi plans to watch the movie with his friend Sam.

2. What would be the correct collective noun for the following?

   (i) A ___________ of elephants.   (ii) A ___________ of sticks.

 (iii) A ___________ of napkins.   (iv) A ___________ of bees.

  (v) A ___________ of wolves.   (vi) A ___________ of cards.

 (vii) A ___________ of grapes.   (viii) A ___________ of goats.

 (ix) A ___________ of sheep.   (x) An ___________ of soldiers.

3. Fill in the blanks using the correct form of abstract nouns.

   (i) Ankita was filled with ___________ (*joyful*) on hearing the good news.

  (ii) On reaching Jim Corbett Park, we immediately set out on a trek with a lot of ___________ (*enthusiastic*).

 (iii) You need ___________ (*determine*) to do well in sports.

 (iv) The elephant has a lot of ___________ (*strong*) in its trunk.

  (v) It was just bad ___________ (*lucky*) that our school lost the game.

4. Match the group of words in Column A to their possessive forms in Column B.

	Column A		Column B
(i)	The hat of the man	(a)	The dogs' collars
(ii)	The dresses of the women	(b)	The cows' horns
(iii)	The hives of the bees	(c)	The man's hat
(iv)	The collars of the dogs	(d)	The women's dresses
(v)	The horns of the cows	(e)	The bees' hives

5. Fill in the blanks with the noun form of the underlined words.

(i) My neighbour <u>arranged</u> a theme party for kids. I liked the ____________ .

(ii) We are <u>celebrating</u> our anniversary today. Will you come for the ____________?

(iii) Rachel loves music and <u>collects</u> CDs. She has a fantastic ____________ .

(iv) Nikhil picked up his brush and <u>painted</u> a picture on the yellow paper. He is good at making ____________ .

(v) Aditi <u>adjusted</u> fast to the new school. She made quick ____________ .

B. Pronouns

6. Fill in the blanks using the correct pronouns from the box given below.

> us, her, him, me, them, you

(i) I can't draw this. Could you help ____________, please?

(ii) Is Surbhi in the photograph? Yes, I can see ____________ .

(iii) You like watches. I bought this watch from a famous shop. It is for ____________ .

(iv) We ordered wood-fried pizzas. Are these for ____________?

(v) Today is Ujjwal's birthday. This cake is for ____________ .

(vi) These are my pets. I love ____________ .

7. Fill in the blanks with appropriate reflexive pronouns from the box given below.

> herself, himself, itself, myself, ourselves, themselves, yourself

(i) Naina bought ____________ a new dress for the festival.

(ii) Rajat met the President ____________ .

(iii) Sooraj is angry with ____________ .

(iv) I solved the puzzle by ____________ .

(v) You must control ____________ and stop shouting at others.

Subject and Predicate

1. Bold the subject and underline the predicate in the following sentences.

   (i) Manu runs a mile every morning.

   (ii) Camels drink a lot of water at one go.

   (iii) I like to drink a glass of milk every day.

   (iv) Arun's mother makes him a heavy breakfast every day.

   (v) Nisha loves chocolates.

   (vi) Our teacher was angry at our behaviour.

   (vii) Some boys are playing in the park.

   (viii) Can you speak English?

2. Rearrange the words to form correct sentences. Remember that the subject is followed by the predicate.

   (i) are/a/hobbies/fun/lot/of

   (ii) popular/collecting/is/a/very/stamp/hobby

   (iii) Nishant/stamps/collects

   (iv) stamps/got/a/lot/he/has/of

   (v) postcards/collects/picture/Surbhi

   (vi) about/has/a/Surbhi/hundred/postcards/picture

3. In each sentence given below, select the correct option.

(i) The professor handed out a syllabus on the first day of class.

The subject (noun) is

(a) professor ☐   (b) syllabus ☐   (c) class ☐

(ii) I broke the zipper on my backpack.
The predicate (verb) is

(a) broke ☐   (b) zipper ☐   (c) backpack ☐

(iii) Typing is an important skill.
The subject is

(a) typing ☐   (b) is ☐   (c) skill ☐

4. Here are some sentences divided into subject and predicate, but the parts are mixed up. Fit the right parts together to make sensible sentences.

Subject	Predicate
(i) The baby	(a) will come to our city tomorrow.
(ii) My cycle	(b) is very beautiful.
(iii) The President	(c) bought a bunch of pink roses.
(iv) People	(d) went to see an old English film.
(v) My mother	(e) may fall and hurt itself.
(vi) Our teacher's hair	(f) is the most popular sport in India.
(vii) Our class	(g) will holiday on the Moon in another ten years.
(viii) Cricket	(h) has a flat tyre.

5. Read the following story about Kriti, who loved chocolates. Then, answer the questions in complete sentences i.e. with subject as well as predicate.

Kriti loved chocolates. One Sunday, her aunt gave her fifty rupees. Kriti quickly ran to a sweet shop. There she bought two bars of chocolate. She ate the chocolates sitting in her garden. Then Kriti's mother called her and asked her to complete her homework. Her mother gave her three bars of chocolate. Kriti quickly ate the bars. Then her mother called her for lunch. Kriti could not eat the special Sunday lunch because she had a stomach ache. She had eaten too many chocolates!

(i) Who loved chocolates?

(ii) What did Kriti's aunt give her?

Chapter 6

Conjunctions

1. Fill in the blanks with the correct conjunction from those given in brackets after each sentence.

   (i) It was a bright sunny day, _____________ white clouds flitted across the sky. (*and/but*)

   (ii) Anil _____________ Riya were walking in the woods _____________ Riya was enjoying the fresh air _____________ Anil was not. (*or/and, and/but, and/but*)

   (iii) Their mother was very worried _____________ upset because they were late. (*or/and*)

   (iv) They had taken some lovely photographs _____________ they showed them to their mother. (*or/and*)

   (v) Their mother was happy to see the photographs _____________ she scolded them for being so late. (*but/or*)

2. Choose the most appropriate conjunction to fill in the blanks.

   (i) The bus stopped _____________ the man got off.
   (a) and ☐ (b) but ☐ (c) or ☐ (d) so ☐

   (ii) We stayed at home _____________ watched a film.
   (a) and ☐ (b) but ☐ (c) or ☐ (d) so ☐

   (iii) I wanted to buy a newspaper _____________ didn't have enough money.
   (a) and ☐ (b) but ☐ (c) or ☐ (d) so ☐

   (iv) I have a lot of homework to do now _____________ I can't go to the cinema with you.
   (a) and ☐ (b) but ☐ (c) or ☐ (d) so ☐

   (v) He's very rich _____________ he doesn't spend a lot of money.
   (a) and ☐ (b) but ☐ (c) or ☐ (d) so ☐

   (vi) Do you want tea _____________ coffee?
   (a) and ☐ (b) but ☐ (c) or ☐ (d) so ☐

3. Fill in the blanks with 'after' or 'before'.

    (i) Lunch comes __________ breakfast.

   (ii) Put on your socks __________ your shoes.

  (iii) In the alphabet series, B comes __________ C.

  (iv) She went to bed __________ she brushed her teeth.

   (v) Please throw the trash away __________ you finish eating.

  (vi) Raise your hand __________ you ask a question in class.

4. Combine each pair of sentences with the conjunction 'and' to make a new sentence. One has been done for you.

    (i) The seagull flew over my head.   The seagull landed on the roof.

        The seagull flew over my head and landed on the roof.

   (ii) My dad drives the boat.   My brother drives the boat.

  (iii) Bobby played hide and seek.   Nina played hide and seek.

  (iv) The dog caught the ball.   The dog brought the ball back to me.

   (v) My friend Meera went to the movie theatre. I went to the movie theatre.

  (vi) The pilot landed the plane.   The pilot opened the door to let the passengers out.

 (vii) Somya painted a picture.   Somya put it on the table to dry.

(viii) Mrs Gupta corrected the spelling tests.   Miss Kohli corrected the spelling tests.

Chapter 7

Prepositions

1. Match the following prepositions in Column A to their usage in Column B.

Column A	Column B
(i) After	(a) To show a higher level or position.
(ii) In	(b) To show the place from where someone or something starts.
(iii) Above	(c) To show the time following an event or action.
(iv) Up	(d) To show a process of using something.
(v) With	(e) In a higher position than something or someone else.
(vi) From	(f) During a period of time.

2. Complete the following passage using suitable prepositions from the box.

> *for, in, along, at, after, to, by, from, on, until*

A Visit to an NGO

Last Friday, our class visited an NGO to see how the NGO serves the community. We left school (i) ___________ 9:00 am and travelled (ii) ___________ one hour (iii) ___________ the bus (iv) ___________ the highway (v) ___________ we reached the main centre located (vi) ___________ KG Marg. (vii) ___________ arrival, we were met (viii) ___________ the Director of the NGO. He took us (ix) ___________ a room where we watched a video (x) ___________ 10:30 am (xi) ___________ 11:30 am. We were allowed to ask questions about what we had seen (xii) ___________ the video. (xiii) ___________ that, we toured the centre to see the various works done by the NGO. We also made a field trip to see the depth of their work. It was the best excursion we have been on this year.

3. There are so many places that a mouse can run to, so that it can escape from a cat! Fill in the blanks from the prepositions given in the brackets.

(i) The mouse can run ___________ (about/in) the house.

(ii) It can jump ___________ (on/onto) the table.

(iii) It can dive _____________ (under/into) the sofa.

(iv) It can sit _____________ (on/onto) the window sill.

(v) It can hide _____________ (under/in) a box.

(vi) It can run _____________ (in/into) its hole!

4. Fill in the blanks with prepositions of time.

(i) We are going to see my parents _____________ the weekend.

(ii) _____________ 1866, a great fire broke out in London.

(iii) My friend has been living in Germany _____________ two years.

(iv) I will have finished this essay _____________ Saturday.

(v) Sidharth is playing tennis _____________ Sunday.

5. Choose the correct preposition from the options given below to fill in the blanks.

(i) The book was written _____________ Mark Twain.

    (a) about   ☐   (b) of ☐

    (c) by   ☐   (d) at ☐

(ii) He reminds me _____________ my old Chemistry teacher.

    (a) about   ☐   (b) of ☐

    (c) from   ☐   (d) on ☐

(iii) The old man met _____________ an accident.

    (a) by   ☐   (b) at ☐

    (c) of   ☐   (d) with ☐

(iv) Many of us eat _____________ fork and spoon.

    (a) from   ☐   (b) by ☐

    (c) of   ☐   (d) with ☐

(v) He arrived at the school building just _____________ time.

    (a) in   ☐   (b) at ☐

    (c) about   ☐   (d) by ☐

(vi) I'll see you _____________ the function.

    (a) at   ☐   (b) on ☐

    (c) in   ☐   (d) about ☐

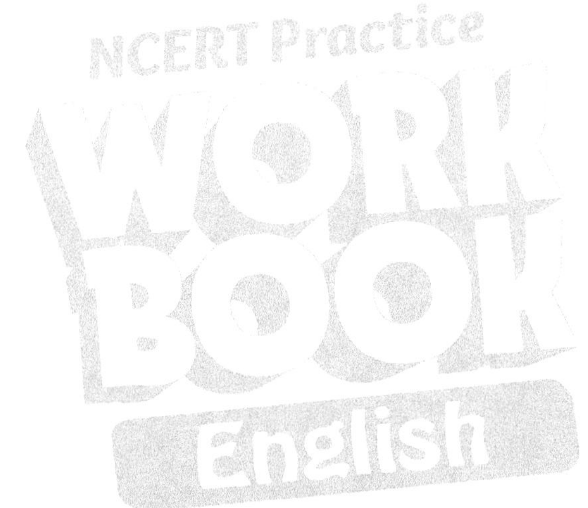

WRITING SKILLS

Chapter 1

Letter Writing

Sample Letter

You are Savita, living at 3244, Navjivan Colony, Mandvi, Mumbai–400032. Your friend Sunayna has shifted to Pune due to her father's transfer. Remembering the sweet memories of the time spent with her earlier, write a letter in about 80 words inviting her to stay with you during the summer vacation. Also, mention what you have planned according to her liking.

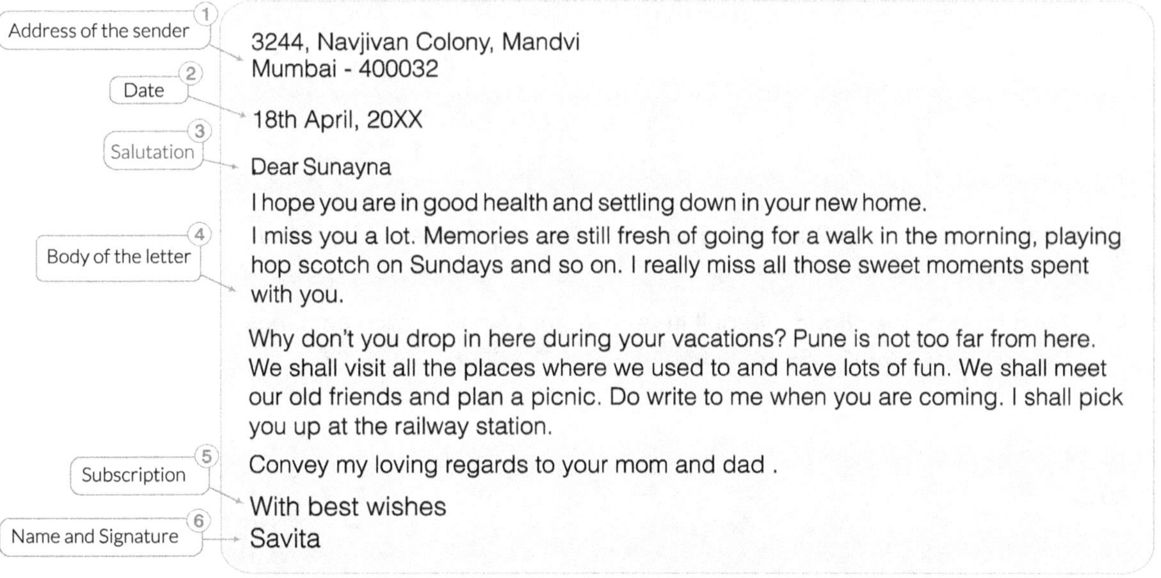

Following points are to be kept in mind while writing a letter:

- Sender's address should be written on the top left hand side of the page.
- Leave a line and then write the date in the next line below the address.
- Leave a line and then write the greeting in the next line.
- Start writing the letter from next line onwards. This is called the body of the letter.
- When you have finished writing the letter, you can leave a line and then write the closing of the letter in the next line.
- You can write your name after leaving a line.

PRACTICE Questions

1. You visited the Amazon river in South America during your summer vacations. Write a letter to your friend in about 80 words describing the different things you saw there. Some clues are given for your help.

> Went on a river trip by boat - Amazon river - largest variety of wildlife - variety of trees and shrubs - home of the Anaconda - largest snake - Piranha - the most ferocious fish - Jaguar - the third largest big cat - a large number of tribes living in the forests

It was great to hear from you after so long. You seem to have had a nice time in Germany. I also had a great time in South America. I …

2. Imagine that you are Shinchan writing a letter to your dear friend Nobhita. Use the following clues and write a letter.

> Mom brought ice-cream – kept it in the refrigerator – not allowed to eat – could not control – ate the ice-cream at night – mom catches and scolds

3. Find out all the important places to visit in and around Delhi and then write about your plan to visit them in a letter to your uncle in Chennai.

4. Sarika recently got her house renovated. Given below are pictures of her house before and after it was renovated.

Imagine yourself as Sarika and write a letter to your cousin describing the changes made in your house.

Chapter 2

Paragraph Writing

Sample Paragraph

☑ *Look at the following sentences. They are from a single paragraph but are not in the correct order. Rewrite the sentences in the correct order in the form of a paragraph.*

   (a) But that day, the teacher asked Ranveer to sit in Rakhi's place.

   (b) Ranveer felt ashamed of himself.

   (c) He liked playing tricks on others.

   (d) When Ranveer sat on her chair, the chewing-gum stuck to his back.

   (e) Ranveer was a very naughty boy.

   (f) One day, Ranveer stuck a chewing-gum on Rakhi's chair.

   (g) Everyone started laughing.

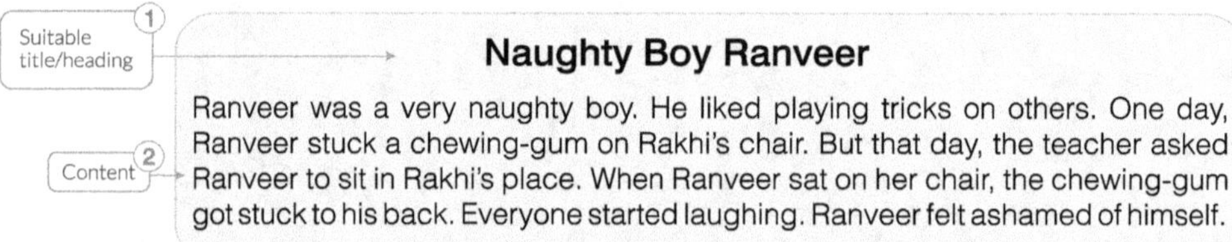

Naughty Boy Ranveer

Ranveer was a very naughty boy. He liked playing tricks on others. One day, Ranveer stuck a chewing-gum on Rakhi's chair. But that day, the teacher asked Ranveer to sit in Rakhi's place. When Ranveer sat on her chair, the chewing-gum got stuck to his back. Everyone started laughing. Ranveer felt ashamed of himself.

Following points are to be kept in mind while writing a paragraph :

* A paragraph should be about a single idea.
* All sentences should contribute to that idea/topic.
* Appropriate sentence linkers should be used to have a well-knit paragraph.

PRACTICE Questions

1. Imagine that you are a tree. Write some of the things that you do for others in a paragraph.

I am a huge, old tree. I provide shelter ____

____

____

____

2. Imagine that you wake up one morning and realise that you have become the size of a fly. Write a short paragraph on what you would do.

____

____

____

____

3. Given below is a paragraph on 'Fairies'. However, some information is missing. Add the missing information from the box given below at the correct places.

presents of food	_true fairies_	_A Boggart_
makes things disappear	_only work at night_	_others are evil_
get away	_kinds of fairies_	_follows them_
some are good	_if anyone is cruel_	_live in our houses_

Fairies

There are different *(i)* ______________. *(ii)* ______________ . Some are mischievous.

(iii) ______________ . *(iv)* ______________ are good. They are very tiny, can fly and do

magic. Brownies are Scottish fairies. They are very tiny and *(v)* ______________ .

Brownies are good. They help around the house, but do not like to be seen, so they

(vi) ______________ . People give them *(vii)* ______________ and they love porridge.

(viii) ______________ to a Brownie, it turns into a Boggart. *(ix)* ______________ is an evil

spirit that *(x)* ______________ . It turns the milk sour and makes dogs lame. Families move

house to *(xi)* ______________ from a Boggart, but the Boggart *(xii)* ______________ .

Chapter 3

Notice Writing

Sample Notice

☑ *You are Parveen, the Cultural Secretary of Gandhi Smarak Primary School, Rohtak. You have been asked to inform all students about taking part in the Annual Day Celebrations with items like Recitation, Speech, Drama, Acting and so on. Draft a notice in not more than 50 words for the notice board giving details. Put the notice in a box.*

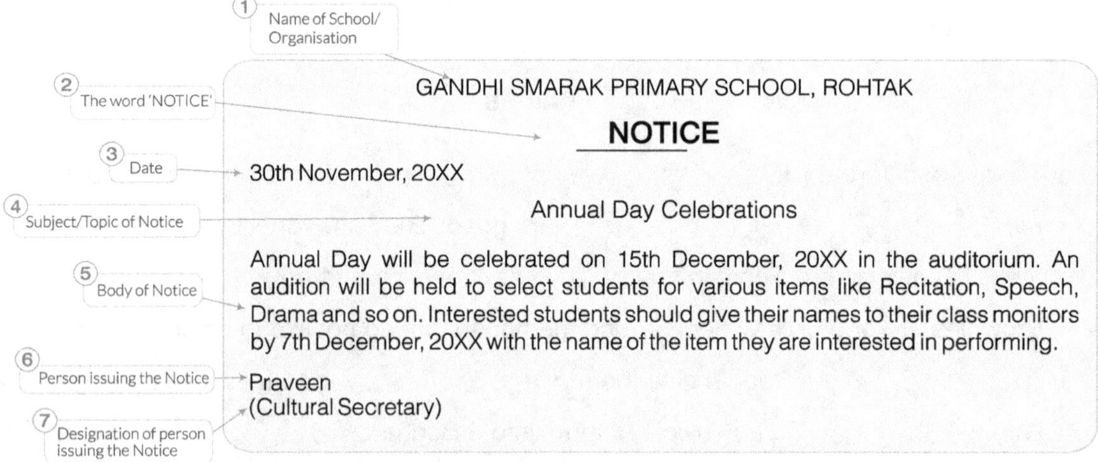

Following points are to be kept in mind while writing a notice

* The entire content of the notice should be enclosed in a box.
* Write the name of the issuing authority in capital letters at the top.
* Write the word 'NOTICE' in capital letters.
* Date of issue of the notice should be mentioned on the left hand side.
* The heading is to be written after the date.
* Mention relevant/eye-catching caption.
* Language of the content should be simple, correct and clear.
* Mention name and designation of the writer at the end of the Notice.
* Notice is written in the third person. Don't use 'I', 'you', etc.

PRACTICE 

1. Write a notice in about 50 words listing the instructions to be followed during the school picnic. Use the following hints if needed

- bus starting time - 8 am from the school
- bus won't wait for latecomers
- trip to a hill station - bring warm clothes, sweaters.
- bring umbrellas - might rain
- bring your mobile phones - if lost - contact class teacher

2. Imagine that you are the Sports Captain of the junior school. Write a notice in about 50 words about an Inter School Football Tournament to be held in your school inviting the students who are interested in participating in it to give their names by 15th September.

3. As Akansha/Aakash, the Junior Head Girl/Boy, complete the notice given below on behalf of your school inviting the grandparents of all the students of your school to celebrate 'Grandparents Day'.

All the students…

4. Your School Coordinator wrote the following notice and gave it to you to put it on the school notice board. However, you spilled some water on it by mistake. As a result, some of the important information got erased. Now complete the missing information from the jumbled notes prepared by your coordinator as rough notes.

Punctuality	Director of the school	expectations	
school inspection	discipline	10th February, 20XX	School
cleanliness	good reputation	School Coordinator	Principal

St Marks School, Shimla
NOTICE

25th January, 20XX

School Inspection

A __________ will be held on __________ by the __________. Students are requested to maintain

__________, __________ and __________ in order to keep up the __________ of your school and live up

to the __________ of your teachers and __________ .

Mrs Kaushik

__________ .

Chapter 4

Story Writing

Sample Short Story

☑ Here is an outline of a popular story. Read it carefully and write the story in your own words.

A grasshopper - loved dancing all day - ant in the garden - taking food into its home - grasshopper asked why it was storing food - replied - storing for winter when no food anywhere - lazy grasshopper - did not bother - continued to dance - winter came - shivered in cold - no food anywhere - went to ant - begged for food - ant refused

Ant and Grasshopper

In a garden there lived an ant and a grasshopper who were very good friends. The grasshopper loved dancing all day. But the ant was hardworking and was collecting food grains and storing them in its house. The grasshopper did not understand why the ant was doing so and asked her why she was storing the food. The ant replied that she was storing the food for the winter when there won't be anything to eat. The grasshopper laughed and did not bother. He continued to dance. When winter came, the grasshopper shivered in cold and did not have any food to eat. It began to starve and went to the ant and begged for food. The ant refused and the grasshopper realised its foolishness.

Following points are to be kept in mind while writing a story:

- The narrative should have a single incident.
- Language should be interesting and effective.
- It should be written in the past tense.
- The story may be fictitious or based on a real life situation.
- As a form of creative art, it should be original.
- Beginning of the story should capture the reader's attention.
- All events should be interconnected.
- There should be a main character in the story.
- The entire narrative should be planned before starting to write.
- A story should have a message for the readers.
- The ending should leave a lasting effect on the readers.

PRACTICE Questions

1. Read the story given below carefully and complete the following gaps with suitable words or phrases.

The frog lived in a _________. The two little frogs took him to a _________ where an _________ was grazing. The frog thought that the _________ was full of air. But he also knew that he wasn't even as big as the _________ . He finally understood that there were others that were _________ than him in the world.

2. Given below is the beginning of a story. Read it and complete the story using your imagination.

Piku was drawing a peacock with her new set of colour pencils. The picture was hardly finished when the peacock suddenly came to life and flew out of the drawing book. Piku was very surprised and also happy. The peacock _________

3. Read the note in the box below. Write a short story (in 80-100 words) about what you think might have happened. The beginning is given for your help. Also give your story a suitable title.

Mr Talwar,
I have both your kids. If you want them back alive, bring ₹ 5 lakh to the hut behind the old railway station at 2 am tonight. Come alone and leave the money under the banyan tree in front of the ancient Hanuman temple. Do not inform the police.

Mr Talwar was very worried. His children, who were playing in the park, had been missing for the past four hours. _________

Chapter 5

Picture Comprehension

Sample Picture Comprehension

☑ Look at the picture given below and answer the questions that follow.

(i) What is the picture about?

Ans. The picture is about a circus show.

(ii) How many animals do you see in the picture? Name them.

Ans. We see two animals in the picture. They are a seal and a lion.

(iii) What are the animals doing?

Ans. The animals are performing tricks.

(iv) What do you find the most interesting in the picture?

Ans. I find the clown holding the balloons very interesting.

(v) What is the girl on the right side of the tent doing?

Ans. The girl is performing some tricks on the rope.

(vi) What are the two clowns doing?

Ans. The clowns are entertaining the audience.

PRACTICE Questions

1. Look at the picture given below and describe it in your own words. Also provide an appropriate title to it.

2. Look at the picture given below and answer the questions that follow.

(i) What is the picture about?

(ii) How many rides can you see in the picture?

(iii) How many children are there on the see-saw?

3. Look at the picture given below and describe it in your own words. Also, give an appropriate title to it.

____

____

____

____

4. Look at the picture given below and describe it in your own words. Also give it a suitable title.

____

____

____

____

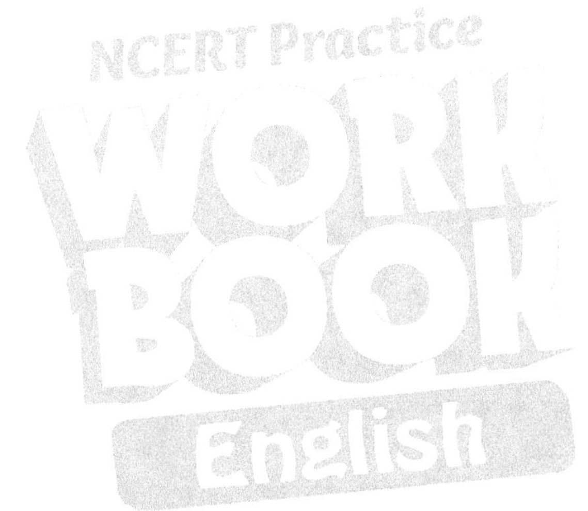

READING
COMPREHENSION

Worksheet 1

1. Read the passage given below and answer the questions that follow.

Television can damage your health. If you sit still for hours at a time, you use a lot less energy than if you are moving. But you don't eat less- in fact, you are likely to eat more- if you watch TV. Most of us like to snack in front of the box. Not only do you eat more when you watch TV, but you also eat the wrong foods: fatty and salty foods such as chips and sugary sweets.

- You eat more and exercise less, so you get fatter.
- You eat unhealthy foods, so you are less healthy.
- You exercise less. This is bad for your heart and other muscles.

There are some good TV programmes – you should choose the one to watch carefully and then switch the TV off afterwards.

Questions

(i) _____________ is bad for our heart and other muscles.

    (a) Eating more food   ☐   (b) Eating less healthy food   ☐

    (c) Less exercise   ☐   (d) Less exercise and more food   ☐

(ii) Find the word from the passage which means the same as 'expected'.

    (a) fact   ☐   (b) also   ☐

    (c) likely   ☐   (d) snack   ☐

(iii) In passage, television is referred to as a box.   ☐ True ☐ False

(iv) Television is harmful for our _____________ .

(v) _____________ and _____________ can be termed as unhealthy foods.

(vi) We get fat when _____________

(vii) What happens when we eat while watching TV?

____

2. Read the poem given below and answer the questions that follow.

The king was sick. His cheek was red,
And his eye was clear and bright;
He ate and drank with a kingly zest,
And peacefully snored at night.
But he said he was sick, and a king should know,
And doctors came by the score;
They did not cure him. He cut off their heads
And sent to the schools for more.

Questions

(i) How did the king punish the doctors who couldn't cure him?

(a) He ate and drank with them

(b) He called them by the score

(c) He cut off their heads

(d) He sent them back to school

(ii) Which of the following words in the poem rhymes with 'bright'?

(a) fat   (b) night

(c) toil   (d) zest

(iii) In the end, the king

(a) cut off his head   (b) called for more doctors

(c) died peacefully   (d) decided to remain sick

(iv) The king used to have a sound sleep at night.   True False

(v) Complete the following sentences.

(a) The king's cheek was ___________ .

(b) The king's eye was ___________ .

(vi) The rhyming scheme of the first stanza is ___________ .

(vii) How did the king eat?

____

Worksheet 2

1. Read the passage given below and answer the questions that follow.

There was once a shepherd boy who used to mind a flock of sheep in the fields. To play a joke on the people in the area, he often used to shout: 'Wolf! Wolf!'

The men working in the fields used to immediately run to his rescue. To their annoyance, they would realise that it was only a trick played on them. But after being cheated two or three times, they decided to take no notice of the boy's shouts.

Soon after, a wolf came and the shepherd boy cried out in earnest. But no one took any notice of his shouts and all his sheep were killed.

Questions

(i) What happened when a wolf came?

    (a) The men came to his rescue

    (b) No one paid attention

    (c) The sheep ran and were killed

    (d) No one took any notice of his shouts and all his sheep were killed

(ii) Find the word from the passage which means the same as 'frustration'.

    (a) rescue

    (b) annoyance

    (c) cheated

    (d) earnest

(iii) The boy always used to play the same joke on the people in the area. | True | False |

(iv) What did the boy do?

____

(v) The men working in the fields used to ____ each time they heard the boy shout.

(vi) The people in the area were cheated _____________________________ .

(vii) How did the boy react when a wolf actually came?

____

2. Read the poem given below and answer the questions that follow.

A Robin Redbreast in a Cage

Puts all Heaven in a Rage.

A Dove house fill'd with doves and pigeons

Shudders Hell thro' all its regions.

A dog starv'd at his Master's Gate

Predicts the ruin of the State

A Skylark wounded in the wing,

A Cherubim does cease to sing.

He who shall hurt the Little Wren

Shall never be beloved by Men.   —*William Blake*

Questions

(i) The Little Wren refers to ____________ .

(a) a singing bird ☐   (b) a hunting bird ☐

(c) a mischievous bird ☐   (d) a notorious bird ☐

(ii) Find the synonym of 'hurt' in the poem.

(a) cease ☐   (b) rage ☐

(c) wounded ☐   (d) wren ☐

(iii) Antonym of 'beloved' is ____________ .

(a) dear ☐   (b) loved ☐

(c) despised ☐   (d) generous ☐

(iv) A man who shall hurt the little bird will never be beloved by men.   True☐ False☐

(v) Which Robin Redbreast put Heaven in a Rage?

____

(vi) Who is wounded in the wing?

____

(vii) What does the Cherubim do?

____

Worksheet 3

1. Read the passage given below and answer the questions that follow.

Why does fear make the hair stand on end? Have you ever been scared of anything? Did it make your hair stand on end? When we are frightened, our hair stands on end like the quills on a porcupine! Do you know why? At the root of the hair we find a tiny muscle. Normally, the hair lies slantwise when the muscle is relaxed. But when the muscle starts working, the hair stands upright!

When we are frightened, our nerves control these tiny muscles and they become active. Thus, the hair is raised. When the hair is upright, a creature actually looks more frightening! A cat, when its hair is standing on end, looks much bigger and more terrible to an enemy.

Questions

(i) The muscles become active

(a) when we are scared

(b) when our nerves control our muscles

(c) when the hair is raised

(d) when the tiny muscles become active

(ii) Find the word in the passage which means the same as 'calm'.

(a) quills   (b) relaxed

(c) control   (d) end

(iii) The hair stands upright when the muscles stop working.   True   False

(iv) The hair stands on end because ____.

(v) When does the hair lie slantwise?

____

(vi) When does a creature looks more scary?

____

(vii) How does a cat look with its hair standing on end?

____

2. Read the poem given below and answer the questions that follow.

I once had a sweet little doll, dears,
The prettiest doll in the world;
Her cheeks were so red and so white; dears,
And her hair so charmingly curled.

But I lost my poor little doll, dears,
As I played in the heath one day;
And I cried for her more than a week, dears;
But I never could find where she lay.

I found my poor little doll, dears,
As I played in the heath one day:
Folks say she's terrible changed, dears,
For her paint is all washed away,

And her arm trodden off by the cows, dears,
And her hair not the least bit curled:
Yet for old sakes' sake she is still, dears,
        The prettiest doll in the world.

Questions

(i) What happened to the doll?

   (a) Her hair had lost its curls

   (b) Her paint was washed away

   (c) Her arm was broken

   (d) All of the above

(ii) The word which rhymes with 'world' is ________________________ .

   (a) dears   (b) curled

   (c) prettiest   (d) day

(iii) The hair of the doll was all messy.   True   False

(iv) The poet could never find her doll.   True   False

(v) The poet had the ________________________ doll in the world.

(vi) The poet ________________________ after she lost her doll.

(vii) Where did the poet lost the doll?

____

Worksheet 4

1. Read the passage given below and answer the questions that follow.

One day a lion was sleeping in the jungle when a mouse ran over its face. The lion woke up and roared and caught the mouse in its paw.

"Please", begged the mouse, "Please don't eat me!"

"Why should I let you go?" said the lion angrily.

"If you let me go, I'll repay your kindness someday", the mouse promised.

The lion found this very funny. How could a small, weak creature like this mouse help the king of the jungle? But because the lion was no longer angry with the mouse, he let it go.

Some weeks later, the lion was chased by hunters and caught in a net. He couldn't move. Suddenly, he heard a scuttling noise and saw the mouse in front of him. The mouse began to gnaw at the ropes of the net. Slowly, it managed to tear away the net and free the lion. The lion was very happy that he had been kind to the mouse earlier.

Questions

(i) How did the mouse repay the lion's kindness?

    (a) He gnawed away the rope of the net and freed the lion ☐

    (b) He untied the rope of the net ☐

    (c) He made a scuttling noise ☐

    (d) He was kind to the lion and helped him ☐

(ii) Find the opposite word of 'strong' from the passage

    (a) beg ☐   (b) weak ☐

    (c) small ☐   (d) funny ☐

(iii) The lion woke up and caught the mouse in its paw.   True False

(iv) "Please don't eat me!"
    (a) Who said this?

____

    (b) To whom?

____

(v) A lion was sleeping in the jungle when ________________________

(vi) What was so funny to the lion?

____

2. Read the poem given below and answer the questions that follow.

The Sun descending in the West,
The evening star does shine;
The Moon, like a flower,
In heaven's high bower,
With silent delight
Sits and smiles on the night.
The feet of angels bright;
Unseen they pour blessing,
And joy without ceasing,
They look in every thoughtless nest,
Where birds are covered warm;
They visit caves of every beast,
To keep them all from harm.
If they see any weeping
That should have been sleeping,
They pour sleep on their head,
And sit down by their bed.

—William Blake

Questions

(i) Here, 'heaven's high bower' means

(a) a potted plant ☐   (b) a framework that supports climbing plants ☐

(c) the sky ☐   (d) a flower vase ☐

(ii) Bird's nest is described as 'thoughtless' because _______________

(a) the angels are blessing the birds to be happy ☐

(b) the birds are covered in the warmth of their nest ☐

(c) it is made without any thought ☐

(d) the occupants are asleep without any care ☐

(iii) The angels come down on the Earth to give blessings and joy. ☐ True ☐ False

(iv) The poet compares Moon to _________________________________.

(v) The angels pour __________ on the birds' head.

(vi) The word 'weeping' as used in the poem means _________________________.

Worksheet 5

1. Read the passage given below and answer the questions that follow.

Do you have to struggle to say, 'She sells sea shells by the sea shore'?

What other tongue-twisters have you tried so far?

Tongue-twisters are sentences that repeat sounds. So, when we try to say them fast, some words get mispronounced. This provides entertainment to those who are listening and all of us can have a good laugh about it. Tongue-twisters also have an important use. By repeating them, we learn to break our words at the correct places, go slow, and enunciate better. They help us to perfect our speech.

You will notice that tongue-twisters are funny, but they do make some sense. They generally repeat the same sound with some break in between by using other connecting words to help the sentence make sense. In 'She sells sea shells by the sea shore' the 'S' and the 'Sh' sound is repeated, and the break is provided by 'by the'.

Questions

(i) How do tongue-twisters make sense?

(a) By repeating the same sound   (b) By using some break in between

(c) By using connecting words   (d) All of these

(ii) The word in the passage which means the opposite of 'mispronounce' is

__________________ .

(a) twister   (b) enunciate

(c) break   (d) perfect

(iii) By repeating tongue-twisters we can perfect our speech.   True   False

(iv) Tongue-twisters provide _______________ to those who are listening and everybody

has a good _______________ .

(v) Tongue twisters are important as

(a) _________________________________ .

(b) _________________________________ .

(c) _________________________________ .

(vi) What are tongue-twisters?

2. Read the poem given below and answer the questions that follow.

I lay in sorrow, deep distress;
  My grief a proud man heard;
  His looks were cold, he gave me gold,
  But not a kindly word.

  My sorrow passed— I paid him back
The gold he gave to me;
Then stood erect and spoke my thanks
And blessed his charity.

I lay in want, and grief, and pain;
  A poor man passed my way,
  He bound my head, he gave me bread,
  He watched me night and day.

How shall I pay him back again
  For all he did to me?
  Oh, gold is great, but greater far
                    Is heavenly sympathy.   *—Charles Mackay*

Questions

  (i) Which of the following statements is not true?

    (a) The poet repaid his debt to the proud man by thanking him.

    (b) The poor man blessed the charity of the poet.

    (c) When the poet was in sorrow he was given money.

    (d) The poet says he cannot repay the poor man for his sympathy.

  (ii) Which word in the poem means 'giving money to a person who is in need'?

    (a) charity   (b) kindness

    (c) sympathy   (d) distress

  (iii) The poor man could not give food to the poet but still took care of him day and night.

                                        True   False

  (iv) The proud man did not give any _________________ to the poet.

  (v) _________________ is far greater than all the gold in the world.

  (vi) How did the proud man help the poet when he was 'in deep distress'?

    ____

Answers

Unit 1

Chapter 1 Wake up

Text Based Questions

1. (iii) (c)   (iv) (d)

2. (i) F   (ii) F   (iii) F   (iv) F   (v) T

Language Based Questions

1. (i) Please   (ii) Buzzing   (iii) Lovely   (iv) Tiniest   (v) Chicken

2. (i) (b)   (ii) (c)   (iii) (a)

Chapter 2 Neha's Alarm Clock

Text Based Questions

1. I. (iv) (b)   II. (iv) (b)

2. (i) T   (ii) F   (iii) F   (iv) F   (v) T

Language Based Questions

1. (i) Alarm   (ii) Unfair   (iii) Smile   (iv) Morning   (v) Escape

2. (i) (d)   (ii) (e)   (iii) (a)   (iv) (b)   (v) (c)

3.

	Before	Missing Word	After
(i)	a	little	longer
(ii)	her	mother's	voice
(iii)	me	up	today
(iv)	I	don't	want

4. (i) Fair   (ii) Remember   (iii) Rise   (iv) Sad   (v) False

Unit 2

Chapter 1 Noses

Text Based Questions

1. I. (iv) (d) (v) (d)   II. (iv) (c)

2. (i) T   (ii) T   (iii) F   (iv) F

Language Based Questions

1. (i) (c)   (ii) (d)   (iii) (e)   (iv) (a)   (v) (b)

2. (i) Sweet   (ii) Foul   (iii) Citrus   (iv) Strong   (v) Chemical   (vi) Fragrant

3. (i) Grows, Shows, Goes   (ii) About, Doubt, Out   (iii) Spare, There

4. (i) looked   (ii) is   (iii) sticks   (iv) wants

Chapter 2   The Little Fir Tree

Text Based Questions

1. I. (iv) (a)   II. (iv) (b)
2. (i) F   (ii) F   (iii) T   (iv) T   (v) F   (vi) F   (vii) F   (viii) F

Language Based Questions

1. (i) (d)   (ii) (e)   (iii) (a)   (iv) (b)   (v) (c)
2. (i) Shelter   (ii) Reward   (iii) Birds   (iv) Morning   (v) Leaves
   (vi) Surprised   (vii) Stole   (viii) Needles
3. (i) Light   (ii) Slow   (iii) Sad   (iv) Dry   (v) Unkind
   (vi) Enemy   (vii) Dull   (viii) Mend/Repair
4. (i) Shetty was a magician.   (ii) It was raining heavily.
   (iii) The fir tree had leaves like needles.

Unit 3

Chapter 1   Run!

Text Based Questions

1. I. (ii) trees   (iii) breeze   II. (iii) grassland

Language Based Questions

1. (i) (b)   (ii) (a)   (iii) (b)   (iv) (c)   (v) (c)
2. (i) from, into, to (ii) in, beneath (iii) down, up, through (iv) through, to
3. Little, Breeze, Hillside, Merry

Chapter 2   Nasruddin's Aim

Text Based Questions

1. I. (iv) (b)   II. (iv) (a)

Language Based Questions

1. (i) (f)   (ii) (h)   (iii) (g)   (iv) (a)   (v) (b)
   (vi) (c)   (vii) (d)   (viii) (e)
2. (ii) Skilfully   (iii) Immediately   (iv) Pointedly
3. (ii) Aim   (iii) Laughter/Laugh   (iv) Defence

Unit 4

Chapter 1   Why?

Text Based Questions

1. I. (iii) Sun, wind   (iv) (b)   (v) (d)   II. (iv) (c)   (v) (c)
2. (i) T   (ii) F   (iii) T   (iv) F   (v) T   (vi) T

Language Based Questions

1. (i) Curious   (ii) Marble   (iii) Cloud   (iv) Reason

2. always, clouds, cross, drink, hard, hills, lead, reason, shine, sink, sun

3. (i) curious, little (ii) sinking   (iii) shining   (iv) blowing   (v) dying

4. (i) Big   (ii) Unknown (iii) Later   (iv) Ahead   (v) Never, Sometimes
   (vi) Easy, Soft (vii) Lost   (viii) Question (ix) Why not

5. (i) Drink   (ii) Die, Why, By, Try

Chapter 2   Alice in Wonderland

Text Based Questions

1. I. (iv) (b)   (v) (c)   II. (iv) (a)   (v) (c)

Language Based Questions

1. (i) (c)   (ii) (a)   (iii) (e)   (iv) (b)   (v) (d)

2.

Size	Colour	Quality	Material
big	white	dry	glass
large	pink	loveliest	
small	blue	bright	
little	red	cool	
	golden		

3. (i) under   (ii) by   (iii) out, from   (iv) down   (v) into

Unit 5

Chapter 1   Don't be Afraid of the Dark

Text Based Questions

1. I. (iii) harsh   (iv) (b)   (v) (b)   II. (iv) (b)   (v) (b)
2. (i) T   (ii) F   (iii) T   (iv) T   (v) T
   (vi) T   (vii) F

Language Based Questions

1. (i) (d)   (ii) (f)   (iii) (a)   (iv) (b)   (v) (g)   (vi) (c)   (vii) (e)
2. (i) dark   (ii) harsh   (iii) troubled   (iv) peaceful
3. (i) EARTH   (ii) SUN   (iii) MOONLIGHT   (iv) STARS   (v) FRIENDS
   (vi) NIGHT   (vii) TRAVEL (viii) TROUBLES   (ix) WORLD   (x) PEACE
4. (i) Done   (ii) Ever   (iii) Near   (iv) Peace
5. (i) Unafraid   (ii) Bright   (iii) Big   (iv) Move   (v) Night
   (vi) Incomplete

Chapter 2   Helen Keller

Text Based Questions

1. I. (iv) (a)   (v) (b)   II. (iv) (a)   (v) (b)

Language Based Questions

1. (i) Summer   (ii) Healthy   (iii) Illness   (iv) Sorry   (v) Teacher

3. (i) (b)   (ii) (e)   (iii) (a)   (iv) (g)   (v) (h)
   (vi) (f)   (vii) (c)   (viii) (d)

4. (i) Healthier, Healthiest   (ii) Smaller, Smallest   (iii) Higher, Highest,
   (iv) Better, Best   (v) Less, Least   (vi) Poorer, Poorest
   (vii) Thicker, Thickest   (viii) Smarter, Smartest   (ix) Wilder, Wildest
   (x) Smarter, Smartest   (xi) Wilder, Wildest   (xii) Dirtier, Dirtiest

5. (i) Unhealthy   (ii) Big   (iii) Hate   (iv) Low

Unit 6

Chapter 1   Hiawatha

Text Based Questions

1. (iv) (b)   (v) (a)

3. (i) built its lodge   (ii) hid its acorns   (iii) ran swiftly   (iv) was very timid

Language Based Questions

1. (i) (b)   (ii) (d)   (iii) (e)   (iv) (f)   (v) (c)   (vi) (g)   (vii) (a)

2. (i) Bottom   (ii) Reveal   (iii) Destroy   (iv) Slow

3. (i) nests   (ii) lodges   (iii) burrows

4. (i) Awl   (ii) Dear   (iii) Meat   (iv) There   (v) Billed

Chapter 2   The Scholar's Mother Tongue

Text Based Questions

1. I. (iii) (d)   (iv) (c)   II. (iv) (a)   (v) (c)

Language Based Questions

2. (i) over   (ii) at   (iii) up   (iv) to, at   (v) into, with

Unit 7

Chapter 1   A Watering Rhyme

Text Based Questions

1. (iii) (b)   (iv) (a)

Language Based Questions

1. (i) (c)   (ii) (d)   (iii) (a)   (iv) (e)   (v) (b)

2. (i) MORNING   (ii) FLOWER   (iii) NOONDAY   (iv) MOUTHS   (v) BOOTS   (vi) EARTH

3. (i) Late   (ii) Low   (iii) Evening   (iv) Live

4. (i) Flower   (ii) Die   (iii) Boots   (iv) Feet

5. (i) ROSE   (ii) LOTUS   (iii) LILY   (iv) JASMINE

Chapter 2 The Giving Tree

Text Based Questions

1. I. (iii) (c) (iv) (a) II. (iv) (b) (v) (c)

Language Based Questions

1. (i) (d) (ii) (a) (iii) (b) (iv) (c) (v) (e)

2. (i) and (ii) and (iii) and (iv) but (v) but

3. (i) by (ii) to (iii) up, from (iv) to (v) in (vi) on (vii) with

4.

	Comparative	Superlative			Comparative	Superlative
(i)	Smaller	Smallest		(ii)	Funnier	Funniest
(iii)	More delicious	Most delicious		(iv)	More tired	Most tired
(v)	Happier	Happiest				

Chapter 3 The Donkey

Text Based Questions

1. (iii) (d) worst

Language Based Questions

1. (i) donkey (ii) wallop (iii) hay (iv) little (v) corn

2. (i) had (ii) would (iii) would find (iv) would give (v) would

3. (i) No (ii) Born

Unit 8

Chapter 1 Books

Text Based Questions

1. (iv) (a) (v) (b)

Language Based Questions

1. (i) (b) (ii) (e) (iii) (a) (iv) (c) (v) (d)

4. (i) Go (ii) Close (iii) Narrow (iv) Short

Chapter 2 Going to Buy a Book

Text Based Questions

1. (iv) (b) (v) run

Language Based Questions

1. (i) happy (ii) small (iii) quiet (iv) fat (v) big

2. (i) One, some (ii) Both (iii) Both (iv) two (v) many (vi) These

3. (i) to (ii) in (iii) at (iv) on (v) on

Chapter 1   The Naughty Boy

Text Based Questions

1. (iv) (c)   (v) (b)

2. (i) F   (ii) T   (iii) T   (iv) T   (v) F   (vi) F

Language Based Questions

1. (i) Scotland   (ii) Naughty   (iii) Merry   (iv) Fourscore   (v) Wondered

2. (i) Naughty   (ii) Hard   (iii) Long   (iv) Merry   (v) Red   (vi) Weighty

Chapter 2   Pinocchio

Text Based Questions

1. I. (iv) (b)   (v) (a)   II. (iv) (d)   (v) (b)

Language Based Questions

1. (i) of   (ii) out   (iii) in   (iv) from

2. (i) heard   (ii) set   (iii) named   (iv) decided, send
      (v) told

3. (ii) Puzzle   (iii) Beginning / Beginner   (iv) Growth   (v) Decision

4. (i) Polite   (ii) Normal / Familiar   (iii) Unsurprised   (iv) Short
      (v) Start   (vi) Flexible   (vii) Truth

5. (i) The old carpenter   (ii) The puppet   (iii) Pinocchio   (iv) Pinocchio

[Grammar]

Chapter 1   Adjectives

1. Correct adjectives are

   (i) inactive   (ii) immodest   (iii) untidy   (iv) immovable
   (v) invalid

2. (i) joyous   (ii) sleeping   (iii) burning   (iv) shameful   (v) missing

3. (i) beautiful   (ii) awful   (iii) ashamed   (iv) unfortunate   (v) proud

4. (i) farthest   (ii) most comfortable   (iii) best   (iv) most beautiful
   (v) elder/eldest

5. (i) best   (ii) worst   (iii) elder   (iv) more modern
   (v) most exciting

6. (i) expensive   (ii) scenic   (iii) comforting, comfortable, comforted   (iv) friendly
   (v) woodish, woody, wooded, wooden

Chapter 2 Articles

1. (i) a, an (ii) a, the (iii) a (iv) A, a, the (v) The

3. (i) the (ii) the (iii) a (iv) the (v) the (vi) the (vii) a

4. (i) the (ii) The (iii) the (iv) a (v) the (vi) the

6.

	Before	Missing	After
(i)	in	a	small
(ii)	near	the	temple
(iii)	had	a	happy
(iv)	among	the	trees
(v)	was	a	simple

Chapter 3 Verbs and Tenses

1. (i) (c) dancing (ii) (c) watching (iii) (b) throwing (iv) (a) packing (v) (b) reading

2. (i) washed (ii) stolen (iii) bitten (iv) took (v) answered (vi) burnt

3. (i) asked (ii) answered (iii) replied (iv) thought (v) got
   (vi) threw (vii) married (viii) invited (ix) was (x) realised

4. (i) (b) (ii) (d) (iii) (a) (iv) (c) (v) (a)

Chapter 4 Nouns and Pronouns

1. (i) Ravi is going to watch the movie Spiderman Returns tomorrow.
   (ii) The movie is running at the new theatre, Cinemax.
   (iii) Cinemax is one of the best theatres in Delhi.
   (iv) This week, Ravi's school is closed for Diwali.
   (v) The movie will be on till next Friday.
   (vi) Ravi plans to watch the movie with his friend Sam.

2. (i) herd (ii) bundle (iii) packet (iv) swarm (v) pack
   (vi) pack (vii) bunch (viii) flock (ix) flock (x) army

3. (i) joy (ii) enthusiasm (iii) determination (iv) strength (v) luck

4. (i) (c) (ii) (d) (iii) (e) (iv) (a) (v) (b)

5. (i) arrangement (ii) celebration (iii) collection (iv) paintings (v) adjustment

6. (i) me (ii) her (iii) you (iv) us (v) him (vi) them

7. (i) herself (ii) himself (iii) himself (iv) myself (v) yourself

Chapter 5 Subject and Predicate

1. (i) **Manu** runs a mile every morning.
   (ii) **Camels** drink a lot of water at one go.
   (iii) **I** like to drink a glass of milk every day.
   (iv) **Arun's mother** makes him a heavy breakfast every day.
   (v) **Nisha** loves chocolates.
   (vi) **Our teacher** was angry at our behaviour.
   (vii) **Some boys** are playing in the park.
   (viii) Can **you** speak English?

2. (i) Hobbies are a lot of fun. (ii) Stamp collecting is a very popular hobby.

(iii) Nishant collects stamps. (iv) He has got a lot of stamps.

(v) Surbhi collects picture postcards. (vi) Surbhi has about a hundred picture postcards.

3. (i) (a) (ii) (a) (iii) (a)

4. (i) (e) (ii) (h) (iii) (a) (iv) (g) (v) (c) (vi) (b) (vii) (d) (viii) (f)

Chapter 6 Conjunctions

1. (i) but (ii) and, and, but (iii) and (iv) and (v) but

2. (i) (a) (ii) (a) (iii) (b) (iv) (d) (v) (b) (vi) (c)

3. (i) after (ii) before (iii) before (iv) after (v) after (vi) before

Chapter 7 Prepositions

1. (i) (c) (ii) (f) (iii) (e) (iv) (a) (v) (d) (vi) (b)

2. (i) at (ii) for (iii) in (iv) along (v) until (vi) on (vii) On

(viii) by (ix) to (x) from (xi) to (xii) in (xiii) After

3. (i) in (ii) onto (iii) under (iv) on (v) in (vi) into

4. (i) over (ii) In (iii) for (iv) by (v) on

5. (i) (c) (ii) (b) (iii) (d) (iv) (d) (v) (a) (vi) (a)

[Writing]

Chapter 2 Paragraph Writing

3. (i) Kinds of fairies (ii) some are good (iii) others are evil

(iv) true fairies (v) live in our houses (vi) only work at night

(vii) presents of food (viii) if anyone is cruel (ix) A Boggart

(x) makes things disappear (xi) get away (xii) follows them

Chapter 3 Notice Writing

4. (i) school inspection (ii) 10th February, 20XX (iii) Director of the school

(iv) discipline (v) cleanliness (vi) punctuality

(vii) good reputation (viii) expectations (ix) School Principal

(x) School Coordinator

[Reading Comprehension]

Worksheet 1

1. Passage

(i) (c) Less exercise (ii) (c) likely (iii) True

(iv) health (v) Fatty, salty foods

(vi) we eat more and exercise less (vii) We eat more while watching TV.

2. **Poem**

    (i) (c) He cut off their heads.   (ii) (b) night   (iii) (b) called for more doctors

    (iv) True (v) (a) red (b) clear and bright   (vi) abcb

    (vii) The king ate with a kingly zest.

Worksheet 2

1. **Passage**

    (i) (d) No one took any notice of his shouts and all his sheep were killed.

    (ii) (b) annoyance   (iii) True

    (iv) The boy used to mind a flock of sheep.

    (v) immediately run to his rescue   (vi) two-three times

    (vii) The boy cried out in earnest.

2. **Poem**

    (i) (a) a singing bird   (ii) (c) wounded   (iii) (c) despised

    (iv) True   (v) The one who is in a cage.

    (vi) The Skylark is wounded in the wing.

    (vii) The Cherubim ceases to sing.

Worksheet 3

1. **Passage**

    (i) (a) when we are scared   (ii) (b) relaxed   (iii) False

    (iv) we are frightened   (v) The hair lie slantwise when the muscle is relaxed.

    (vi) A creature looks more scary when the hair is upright.

    (vii) It looks much bigger and more terrible to an enemy.

2. **Poem**

    (i) (d) All of the above   (ii) (b) curled   (iii) False

    (iv) False   (v) prettiest   (vi) cried for more than a week

    (vii) The poet lost the doll while playing in the heath.

Worksheet 4

1. **Passage**

    (i) (a) He gnawed away the rope of the net and freed the lion   (ii) (b) weak

    (iii) True   (iv) (a) The Mouse (b) The Lion (v) a mouse ran over its face

    (vi) When the mouse promised to repay the lion's kindness if he (the lion) let him go, the lion found it funny.

2. **Poem**

    (i) (c) the sky   (ii) (d) the occupants are asleep without any care

    (iii) True   (iv) a flower   (v) sleep

    (vi) crying

Worksheet 5

1. Passage

(i) (d) All of these   (ii) (b) enunciate   (iii) True

(iv) entertainment, laugh

(v) (a) We learn to break words at the correct places.

(b) We learn to speak slowly.   (c) We can enunciate better.

(vi) Tongue twisters are sentences that repeat sounds.

2. Poem

(i) (b) The poor man blessed the charity of the poet.   (ii) (a) charity   (iii) False

(iv) sympathy   (v) Heavenly sympathy

(vi) The proud man gave him some money when he was 'in deep distress.'